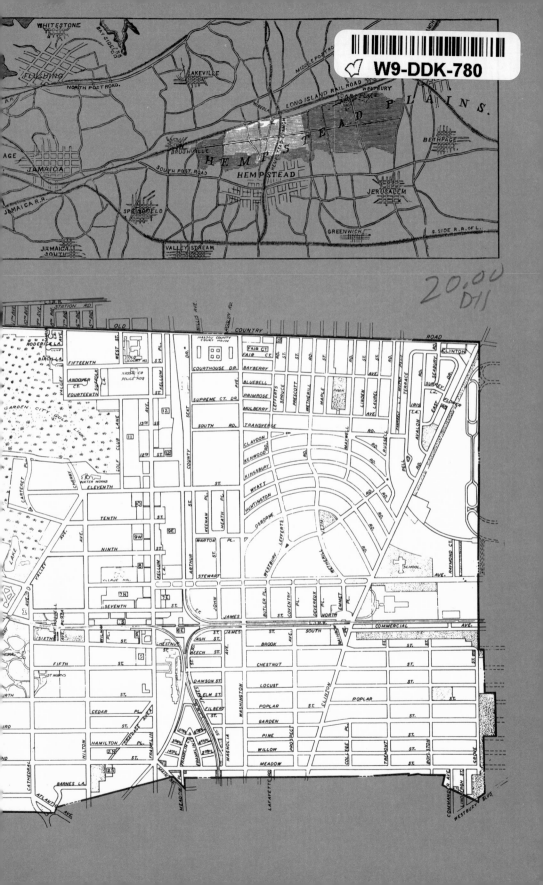

20.00
D11

HISTORY OF GARDEN CITY

HISTORY OF

GARDEN CITY

REVISED EDITION

by

M. H. SMITH

GARDEN CITY HISTORICAL SOCIETY

HISTORY OF GARDEN CITY

First Edition: 1963, Channel Press

Revised Edition: Copyright © 1980 by Garden City Historical Society

Library of Congress Catalog Card Number: 80-1700

International Standard Book Number: 0-9604654-0-5

CONTENTS

A NOTE OF THANKS

The Garden City Historical Society would like to thank:
Doubleday & Company, Inc.
The Long Island Trust Company
The Incorporated Village of Garden City
Adelphi University
The Estates, Central and Eastern Property Owners
Associations of Garden City
whose grants have made possible the publication of this revised edition
of *The History of Garden City*.

FOREWORD

Garden City, roughly nineteen miles from New York City, is lo-
cated in the western section of central Nassau County in the Town-
ship of Hempstead, Long Island, New York. It is ninety feet above sea-
level, and covers 3,390 acres, or approximately 5.3 square miles. On
the north it is bounded by New Hyde Park, Garden City Park, Mine-
ola and Carle Place; on the east by unincorporated areas of the Town
of Hempstead, comprising Roosevelt Field Shopping Center and
what was once Mitchel Field; on the south by Hempstead, West
Hempstead, Munson and Franklin Square; and on the west by Stew-
art Manor and New Hyde Park. It is basically coterminous with
School District No. 18.

Founded by Alexander Turney Stewart over one hundred years
ago on the uninhabited and treeless Hempstead Plains, Garden City
now has a population of just over 25,000, and is famous for its at-
tractive homes, parks, and great avenues of trees. The history that fol-
lows tells the story of this unique American village, which was de-
liberately planned from the start and has successfully realized the
ideals of its founder.

M. H. SMITH
Village Historian

1

THE HEMPSTEAD PLAINS

Almost overnight, in the early eighteen seventies, the Village of Garden City sprang into being on the treeless Hempstead Plains. It was surprising enough that one of the wealthiest men in the country should have decided to create this village on Long Island, but the location which he chose was even more surprising.

The Hempstead Plains, lying in the central section of western Long Island, had been a matter of curiosity and conjecture from the beginning of recorded history in the New World, and had deteriorated into thousands of acres of neglected waste land at the time of their sudden purchase in 1869 by Alexander Turney Stewart.

As far back as 1670, Daniel Denton, in his *Brief Description of New York*, wrote: "Towards the middle of Long-Island lyeth a plain sixteen miles long and four broad, upon which plain grows very fine grass, that makes exceeding good Hay, and is very good pasture for sheep and other Cattel." In 1759 the Rev. Burnaby visited the Plains and said that they were "between twenty and thirty miles long, and four or five miles broad; and . . . there was not a tree then growing upon them." He went on to add that "strangers are always carried to see this place, as a great curiosity, and the only one of the kind in

North America." Thirty years later, in 1790, George Washington wrote in his journal: "We left Jamaica about eight o'clock, and pursued the road to South Hempstead, passing through the South edge of the plain by that name . . . without a tree or shrub growing on it. At the few settlements thereon, the soil of this plain is said to be thin and cold and of course not productive." And as late as 1810 Timothy Dwight, late president of Yale College, after traveling through the Plains, used such descriptive terms as "it is the Easternmost of those 'American Prairies'; . . . the appearance of its border strongly resembles that of a lake; . . . its vegetation is nothing but a coarse wild grass, which supplies indifferent pasturage for a great number of cattle."

The origins of this Hempstead Plain and of the even larger bushy and scrub oak plains of Suffolk, go back to the days of the glaciers, the last of which formed Long Island as it is today. Ralph Henry Gabriel conveniently condenses these geological facts in his *Evolution of Long Island:* "Not once but four times did Long Island feel the creep of these great glaciers. Hundreds of years at a time the region lay underneath or at the edge of these ice masses loaded with rock and gravel that had been picked up to the northward. . . . The greatest changes were made by the Wisconsin Ice. Twice this broad glacier advanced its southern edge to the top of the Long Island hills and stopped. Each time it built a high ridge of terminal moraine . . . and south of each of these ridges sloped the gently dipping sands and gravels of glacial outwash. The moraines form the present hills of the region, the 'backbone of Long Island.' . . . The outwash plains make up the flat country . . . which slopes gradually to an irregular coastline."

Due to the type of close-packed outwash, the Hempstead Plains, 80 to 100 feet above sea level, developed into prairie or grass plains, whereas the Suffolk plains became wooded or bushy. Grassy or bushy, the Plains were used chiefly for hunting by the Indians of Long Island, who for their settlements much preferred the wooded hilly north shore areas and the coastal land-locked bay areas on the southern shore.

In the sixteen forties, when English settlers crossed the Sound to Long Island from previous New England settlements, they too preferred the shore areas for their villages. One group, however, from the Wethersfield and Stamford areas, after sending emissaries ahead to obtain rights from the Indians to the wide strip of land which now comprises North Hempstead and Hempstead Townships, chose to settle on the southern edge of the great grassy plain that Daniel Denton described. Denton and his father, the Rev. Richard Denton, were among the original settlers who started the little "Town Spot" of Hempstead Village with its streams and ponds to the west and south, and the great plains to the north.

In 1644, the Hempstead settlers received a patent issued by William Kierst, then Governor of the Dutch province of New Netherlands, confirming their rights to the land described as "lying and being upon and about a certain place called the Great Plaines of Long Island, from the East River [the Sound] to the South Sea." Soon other settlers came from New England to found villages on the north shore areas and on the northern edge of the Plains, which were held by the entire Township as common pasturage.

Before very long the Plains were also being used for course racing. As early as 1665, after the Dutch had been superseded by the English, Governor Richard Nicolls instituted the New Market Race Course to the northwest of Hempstead Village (probably around the New Hyde Park Road, Clinch Avenue and Newmarket Road area of today's Garden City). It was here, according to Denton, that "once a year the best Horses in the Island are brought hither to try their swiftness, and the swiftest rewarded with a silver Cup, two being Annually procured for the purpose." After Denton's time, races were held far more frequently and for higher stakes, enthusiasts coming by stage, carriage and horseback from all over the Island to participate.

The Revolution brought an abrupt change, due to the victories of the British and their seven-year occupation of the Island. The Hempstead Plains, stripped of all but a remnant of its large herds of cattle, were soon being used for the quartering and drilling of troops. British officers discovered that Sammis' Tavern in Hempstead Village was a comfortable place for headquarters, and that nearby New Market Course could be an excellent place for relaxation and pleasure. Loyalists, British officers and officials from New York, Brooklyn and outlying posts, flocked to the track during these years to compete or lay their wagers. A notice of Nov. 6, 1779 reads: "New Market Races, Hempstead Plains, on Wednesday; a purse of 20 guineas; the best of three two-mile circular heats. . . . A match between the noted horse

Dulcimore and the roan gelding Kettlebander, for 400 guineas, two miles. God save the King!"

The defeat of the British and their eventual departure left the Island townships in a confused and impoverished state. Hempstead Township suffered particularly, not only because its cattle had been confiscated, but because its citizens had been divided in their loyalties, the northern villages having been solidly on the side of the Revolutionists and the southern villages on that of the British. By 1784 feeling ran so high that the Township was divided into two separate townships by the Legislature of the State of New York—North Hempstead and South Hempstead, the Plains being allotted years later, in 1828, to the latter.

South Hempstead Township, or Hempstead Township as it was subsequently called, was slow in regaining its vigor. Many citizens fled from the area as loyalist refugees, and those that remained worked to reclaim the neglected farms and shipyards. Little by little new families moved in, and growth and prosperity returned. Cattle raising and grazing were continued on the Plains, but at a slower pace; and with the opening of the West's great prairies, they finally declined and died out completely.

Course racing continued at New Market Course, but it also was affected by the strain of post-war conditions. There is some evidence that the track was moved nearer to Queens County Court House, then on Jericho Turnpike and Herricks Road, in the early 1800's. Later it was moved again to East New York, where it became the famous Union Race Track.

But with the decline of New Market Course, the one-mile Washington Course, just north of Hempstead Village, became the popular local track. It was located in what is now Central Garden City, between Rockaway Road and Cathedral Avenue, just south of First Street; and it was here that the famous "Huckleberry Frolics," as well as the races, took place. Thomas Floyd-Jones, in his *Backward Glances*, remembers that "it was on the open prairie, no fence enclosing it, so admittance was free. The purses were made up by someone passing around in the crowd with a tumbler, in which they would put either one, two or four shillings, which would probably amount to ten or twelve dollars. They would trot for the whole afternoon and often away past sundown. Horses would come from Brooklyn, Babylon,

12

The Hempstead Plains

Huntington and other distant places on the Island. . . . The judges' stand on this track was very crude, it being two stories, about six feet square, the bar occupying the ground floor. After each heat the crowd was supposed to "licker up," the drink being gin and sugar, rum or brandy. After the races everyone would go for his horse and wagon, and a merry scramble was had by those going to Hempstead, to get to Steve Hewlett's Hotel on the corner of Main Street first."

Horses, cattle and sheep were still familiar sights on the Plains when in 1834 a new use was found for the flat unbroken miles of prairie land. In that year the Long Island Rail Road was incorporated by special act of Legislature to build a steam railroad from Brooklyn to Greenport. The route chosen for it was through the center of the Island—most of the way through the Hempstead grass plains and the Suffolk scrub oak plains beyond—the quickest and easiest to build for the purpose in hand, which was a railroad link between New York and Boston. The plan was to use the train to Greenport, steamboats to Stonington, Conn., and the Old Colony Railroad to Boston. This "through route" was finished in 1844, and for four years the "Boston" trains ran through the tall waving grass of the Hempstead Plains carrying freight and passengers between the two big cities. There was one "accommodation" train, going east one day and west the next, for Long Islanders to use; and in 1840 a short branch was opened to Hempstead Village from Hempstead Branch (Mineola) on the main line. It ran south on the roadbed that is still being used for freight, as far as "Hempstead Crossing" in Garden City. It then ran straight through what is now Franklin Court and down the middle of Main Street in Hempstead, to terminate at a small depot between Fulton Avenue and Centre Street. For the first few years a small "dummy" steam locomotive pulled one or two coach-like cars back and forth on this branch. When the Boston connection failed in 1850 and hard times hit the railroad, horses were used to pull the cars; and later still a small engine, looking like an elongated street car, chugged over the branch tracks.

Locomotive "Post Boy," weighing 7 tons and costing $7,000, used by the L.I.R.R. from 1836 to 1852.

2

THE PURCHASE

By 1860 Hempstead Village, serviced by this train and connected with Jamaica and the shore villages by roads and turnpikes, had become not only a thriving and attractive village, but also the seat of government of Hempstead Township. Its beautiful churches served the large area to the south, and it boasted a seminary, Hoffman's Private School, the Long Island Academy, a district school, many handsome houses and farms, a bank, lumber and coal yards, several hotels and inns, a fire brigade, well kept roads, and even gas lamps. The empty plains to the north were serving no good purpose by this time, and were often something of a fire hazard—in fact, according to *The Hempstead Sentinel,* one of Hempstead's two newspapers, they "were become a deserted waste reproaching the torpid energies of the people."

Something had to be done, and during that year various suggestions and plans were made and hotly discussed in Hempstead Town meetings. One of these was to divide the land in equal portions among the voters of the Town. This was quickly hailed by many, but calmer citizens felt that the plan would be too complicated in that it would entail registration of voters, a bill to be put before the Legisla-

14

ture for the survey and disposal of the land, a commission to carry out the plan, and funds to defray the costs.

Another plan proposed the mapping and open sale of the land, the proceeds to be used for the public good. This suggestion met with loud protests from a minority group which felt that the sale of the lands was akin to confiscation:—"let them sell the Plains, and then the marshes will go, and the next they'll sell your farms."

But the majority of citizens felt differently and eventually adopted the plan as the most sensible and democratic solution to their problem. Although the State Legislature authorized the appointment of commissioners as early as 1862, nothing was done until 1867, when it passed an act (Laws of the State of New York, Chapter 639) authorizing "The Freeholders and Electors of the Town of Hempstead, Queens County, the State of New York, to sell their common lands, or any portion thereof."

The Plains were now for sale, but it was not until 1869 that Charles T. Harvey made an offer to buy the bulk of the Plains at $42 an acre. Even before the special Town meeting could be held to vote on the sale, a higher offer of $55 an acre, "the entire purchase to be paid in Cash," was made by a New York merchant, A. T. Stewart.

Alexander Turney Stewart, "one of the richest merchants of the world," according to *The New York Times,* was a man of sixty-six at this time. Born in Ireland on October 12, 1803,[1] of Scotch Protestant parentage, he had spent his youth in that country until 1820, when he came to New York to see the world and to make his fortune. After teaching for a year, and making a quick round trip to Ireland to claim a $10,000 inheritance, he settled down in his adopted city and started a small retail dry-goods business on the ground floor of a narrow clapboard house on lower Broadway. This was also to be his first home, to which he brought his young wife, Cornelia Mitchell Clinch, daughter of a well-to-do ship chandler, after their marriage on October 16, 1823.

Stewart had an instinct for trade, and the business, consisting largely of imported laces, ribbons, trimmings, and linen, was an immediate success. Working late hours, saving every penny, sticking

[1] Some reliable sources now suggest that he was actually born two years earlier, on October 12, 1801.

Alexander Turney Stewart, multi-millionaire
merchant, who founded, built, and completely owned
and operated Garden City from his purchase
of the Plains in 1869 until his
death in 1876.

to a "strictly cash" basis, and innovating such new selling angles as the fire and remnant sales, he built up his business so rapidly that he was soon able to move to larger quarters. Within ten years he moved again, to Broadway and City Hall Park, into his own store, which was so elegant and handsome that it was called the Marble Dry Goods Palace. Undisputed leader in merchandising in 1862, he then bought a large tract of land on Tenth Street, where he built the Great Iron Store which was later to become John Wanamaker's. John Kellum had been the architect of this palatial store, and he now designed Mr. Stewart's mansion on Fifth Avenue and 34th Street. This was known to New Yorkers as the Marble Palace; and those lucky enough to be invited to Mr. Stewart's formal Sunday suppers could admire the rich furnishings of the large high-ceilinged rooms, and exclaim over the large canvases and draped statuary that formed part of their host's million-dollar art collection. In fact, although a small and retiring man, Mr. Stewart, in all phases of his life and career, chose to do things on a large scale. His holdings in New York City and elsewhere followed this pattern and included, besides the two stores, the Metropolitan and Park Hotels, the Globe Theatre, Niblo's Garden, the Grand Union Hotel in Saratoga, and "more New York City real estate than any man except William Astor."

By 1869, at the end of the Civil War, his wealth had increased to such a point that he was ready for a new project. Unable to secure confirmation to the cabinet post of Secretary of the Treasury in the Grant administration because of his vast business interests, his attention was attracted to the seven-thousand-acre tract which was now for sale on Long Island. John Kellum, his architect, had been born in Hempstead, and undoubtedly suggested its purchase as a further excellent real estate investment. Its very size, more than two-thirds the area of Manhattan, must have appealed to Mr. Stewart even more than its other possibilities.

His offer of $55 per acre for the Plains caused a sensation in Hempstead Township, the price being so much more than that offered by Mr. Harvey and so much more than the land was held to be worth. Worse yet, rumors were rife that Mr. Stewart was planning to develop the land for tenements and public charities. Doubt in fact ran so high that *The Sentinel* had to reassure its readers editorially: "There is no mistake, the offer is made in good faith by Mr. Stewart

—he is willing to expend *several millions of dollars* in improving the Plain land; . . . the sum looks amazingly large, but he has the means and will do it if he says so." Mr. Stewart himself wrote a letter to the Town promising to develop the land for actual settlers and to erect attractive buildings and residences, so that, as he said, "the barren waste may speedily be covered by a population desirable in every respect."

Excitement ran high, and Pettit's Hotel did a record business on July 17, 1869, when the citizens of Hempstead Town came to vote on the sale of their lands. According to *The Sentinel*, "the day was very pleasant, and there was a good vote taken, the number of ballots cast being 1,138, of which 1,077 were in favor of accepting Mr. Stewart's offer, and 52 for Mr. Harvey's, and 9 were what is called scattering." The 'scattering' referred to later offers, and in no wise detracted from Mr. Stewart's victory.

During the next two months the unfortunate Mr. Harvey made various claims and used every means to restrain the Supervisor from delivering the deed. But through the efforts of Judge Henry Hilton, Stewart's advisor and counsel, the conveyance of the property was finally effected, and the deed for the sale of 7,170 acres (exclusive of roads) of the Hempstead Plains, for $394,350, was recorded on Sept. 13, 1869, at the office of the County Clerk in Jamaica. Stamps on the conveyance nearly covered the entire paper, and cost $3,944. By Act of Legislature the money was to be invested—two-thirds of the proceeds to be devoted to educational purposes in the Township and one-third to the support of the poor.

Besides the 7,170 acres, Mr. Stewart subsequently purchased over 2,000 acres more from individual land owners to round out his property, which extended roughly through the Plains from Floral Park to Bethpage.

Notice of Hempstead Town Meeting,
called to vote on the proposed sale
of the Hempstead Plains.
Mr. Stewart's last-minute offer of
$55 an acre necessitated
a write-in vote.

SPECIAL TOWN MEETING.

To the Supervisor of the Town of Hempstead, Queens County:—

We, the undersigned, Electors and Freeholders of the Town of Hempstead, having learned, and believing it to be true, that an offer of Forty-two Dollars per acre has been made for the Common lands, known as the Plains, embraced within a recent survey, made under the direction of the Town Board of said Town,

Now, therefore, we, your petitioners, request that you call a Special Town Meeting, to determine, by ballot, whether said Plain Lands shall be sold for said price or sum, or not.

J. A. White	W. B. Snedeker	John B. Pettit	John Malganson	Birdsall Post	Mott Wood
John B. Pettit	Coles Carman	John R. Anderton	Benjamin K. Smith	John B. Seats	Lott Van De Water
James Bedell	Elbert Cooper	Abraham Bedell	Lewis W. Angevine	Nelson H. Duryea	Samuel L. Pettit
Lattoe Smith	Lockwood Abrams	Treadwell Pearsall	Elbert Rushmore	Alfred Wilmarth	Judah H. Miller
William Stoffel	Samuel K. Searing	B. F. Rushmore	Townsend B. Pettit	Wm. M. Carmichael	J. J. A. Morgan
John H. Curtis	O. D. Lane	R. G. Powell	A. R. Hunt	Ebenezer Kellum	Abram Cornwell
Thomas Seaman	R. O. Gildersleeve	Cornelius B. Adams	Vandewater Smith	Cornelius Vandewater	Noah Jackson
Robert Wood	John Flower	G. N. Searing	Samuel Riley	Henry Bedell	Joseph Mott
A. R. Griffin	James H. Nichols	M. J. Gildersleeve	Thomas H. Clowes	Frederick Rowland	John B. Post
Stephen Powell	Henry S. Nichols	Daniel Clark	George Willets	William H. Hawkins	Henry Walters
John R. Bedell	George Duryea	E. W. Brueninghausen	Jacob Valentine	William Golder	C. Snedeker
James G. Cornell	Zebulon Pinkham	H. P. Seabury	S. M. Gildersleeve	Samuel K. Minshull	Benjamin A. Raff
Carman Lush	William M. Akley	John Harold	Sanda Powell	Q. A. Sammis	A. V. Cortelyou
Caleb Van Law	Sanda Powell	T. N. Eldert	Charles B. Everitt	M. Snedeker	Jonathan T. Mobby
Michael Coon	George N. Paff	Thomas C. Weekes	Thomas F. Gilbert	Nathaniel Smith	S. M. Pine
S. H. Gildersleeve	Arrender Smith	Henry Powell	Robert Van De Water	Thomas Dauch	Charles Orowman
Charles A. Powell	Oliver Hendrickson	George E. Rockenbell	Lawrence Wood	Edwin Webb	William Raynor
James Lush	John P. Wright	Isaac Daffotti			

I, Carman Cornelius, Supervisor of the Town of Hempstead, Queens County, N. Y., by virtue of the foregoing requisition, order and direct that a SPECIAL TOWN MEETING of the Electors of said Town, be called on SATURDAY, THE 17th DAY OF JULY, 1869, to consider and determine, by ballot, in accordance with special enactments of the Legislature of the State of New York, authorizing the Freeholders and Electors of said Town of Hempstead to sell their common lands or any portion thereof.

Dated June 26, 1869.

CARMAN CORNELIUS, Supervisor.

To J. Merwin Oldrin, Town Clerk of the said Town of Hempstead.

Now, therefore, *Whereas*, Chapter 639 of the Laws of the State of New York, passed April 23, 1867, authorizes the Freeholders and Electors of the Town of Hempstead, Queens County, and State of New York, to sell their Common Lands, or any portion thereof, and

Whereas, A resolution was passed at the last general Town Meeting of said Town, held April 6, 1869, authorizing and ordering the Commissioners of said Town (elected at a Special Town Meeting, held January 5, 1869, for the purpose of electing Commissioners for the sale of that portion of their Common Lands, called the Hempstead Plains, authorized by virtue of Chapter 350 of the Laws of the State of New York, passed April 19, 1862,) to sell the aforesaid Plain Lands in one parcel, instead of sections, and

Whereas, An offer of Forty-two Dollars per acre has been made, and an agreement entered into by the said Commissioners, together with the Supervisor and Town Clerk of said Town, with one Charles T. Harvey, subject to the approval by a vote of the Freeholders and Electors of said Town,

Now, therefore, I, J. Merwin Oldrin, Town Clerk of said Town of Hempstead, give notice that

A Special Town Meeting

WILL BE HELD AT THE

HOUSE OF JOHN B. PETTIT,

IN THE VILLAGE OF HEMPSTEAD, ON

Saturday, July 17th, 1869,

Commencing at 7 o'clock, A. M., and closing at sunset, for the purpose of determining, by ballot, as aforesaid, whether said offer shall be accepted, and said Plain Lands be conveyed as expressed in said agreement or not, for said sum of Forty-two Dollars per acre.

Dated June 26th, 1869.

J. MERWIN OLDRIN, Town Clerk.

3

MR. STEWART'S GARDEN CITY

Once in possession of the land, Mr. Stewart lost no time in publishing his elaborate plans for the entire area and for the model village which, with himself at the helm, was to be its center, and which would provide "pleasant and reasonable" housing on the rental basis, for the executives and clerks who worked in his stores and in other similar business houses. Stewart was to own and operate the entire village with all its facilities, and to be in control of its policies and development.

The press and public were greatly impressed by this grandiose scheme. *Harper's Weekly* piously wrote: "The design is so gigantic that it throws into the shade every attempt of the kind hitherto made. . . . Hempstead Plain, hitherto a desert, will be made to bloom as a rose; it will be the most beautiful suburb in the vicinity of New York. God speed the undertaking!"

Later, the historian Peter Ross was to write that Mr. Stewart had conceived the idea "of erecting a Town which would be a model community, a little republic; . . . that everything would be hedged about with restrictions and the place would be exclusive and refined —a veritable Eden."

But not all contemporary opinion was favorable. In a carping mood, *The World* in an 1870 issue expressed itself bluntly: "His purchase of Hempstead Plains, simply because it was the cheapest large property near New York, is certainly against the judgment of real estate operators. He is attempting a daring experiment, nothing less than a community which should have churches, schools, water, gas and all the appliances of municipal life, without a single other person having interest in a foot of the whole domain. He proposes to be landlord, mayor and alderman, in fact the whole municipality. All inhabitants pay him rent and purchase goods at his stores. This may succeed, but it would be a miracle should it do so."

Impervious to the publicity he was getting, Mr. Stewart and his architect, John Kellum, surveyed and mapped out the project. The village proper, comprising 500 acres, was to be located between Mineola and Hempstead, just west of the existing Long Island Rail Road branch that ran between the two villages. It was to have a thirty-acre park, landscaped with winding paths, surrounding a handsome square building which was to serve as the Stewarts' home when they were on Long Island and also as a small hotel with rooms for about 25 guests. The hotel with its park was to be the hub of the Village, and around it an orderly geometric pattern of wide streets was to be laid out for the houses, stores, and other public buildings planned for the community. Existing roads were to be improved and others built, not only in the Village, but to the north and south shores, to provide carriage drives and easy access to other towns. To the east of the railroad, truck farms and gardens were to be laid out, and at Farmingdale a brickyard was to be started for providing material for the larger buildings.

Before developing any of these plans, Mr. Stewart in 1870 moved a small public cemetery, which was east of the proposed village, to a new 20-acre site south of Hempstead, called Greenfield. This he bought, fenced, planted and deeded to the Town of Hempstead, and later had the bodies moved and reinterred.

Railroad facilities for bringing supplies and materials for grading, building and landscaping his village, were Mr. Stewart's next concern. The existing Mineola-to-Hempstead Branch of the Long Island Rail Road would perhaps serve temporarily, but Mr. Stewart felt that his long-range plans called for a branch line of his own to be built through the center of his entire tract from Floral Park to Bethpage.

At this time Oliver Charlick was President of the Long Island Rail Road, which in 1870 still consisted only of the original main line from Brooklyn to Greenport, with branches to Glen Cove, Hempstead, Northport, and Sag Harbor. Charlick, on coming to office seven years before, had ignored the pleas of the other shore villages for railroad facilities, and had been so uncooperative that they had begun building railroads of their own. In this way two new rival railroad systems were developing on the Island—one the South Side system that ran through the south shore villages as far as Patchogue, and the other the North Side system which serviced Flushing and north shore towns as far as Great Neck. Approached by Mr. Stewart, Mr. Charlick, already operating an unremunerative railroad through the uninhabited center of the Island, refused to cooperate with him in any further building program, and feeling that he had Stewart in his power, demanded high rates for the proposed hauling and trucking of materials for the new village.

Determined to solve his problem more favorably, Stewart negotiated with one of Charlick's rivals, the North Side system, and in 1871 a contract was drawn up between the Flushing and North Side Rail Road Company on the one part, and Alexander T. Stewart on the other part, for the construction and operation of a new branch railroad through Mr. Stewart's tract of land. It was to be called the Central Railroad Company of Long Island, and was to run over the North Side system's tracks from Long Island City to Flushing. There the new line would branch off in a south-easterly direction through Rocky Hill to Creedmoor and to what is now Floral Park, cross the Long Island Rail Road's main line by means of an iron bridge, and run to the center of the new village of Garden City. Here it would cross the Long Island Rail Road's branch to Hempstead, and continue east through the Plains to Bethpage.

The line, popularly known as the Stewart Road, cost $66,356 per mile to build. It was finished in 1873 and followed the original plan exactly, providing stations at Creedmoor Rifle Range and Floral Park, but catering chiefly to Garden City, where Mr. Stewart built a compact brick mansard-roofed station as well as a large freight station between Hilton and Franklin Avenues on Sixth Street. The terminal station was at Bethpage, and a small spur ran beyond it to Mr. Stewart's brickworks.

The first Garden City Hotel,
completed in 1874, was also
used by Mr. and Mrs. Stewart
as their Garden City residence.

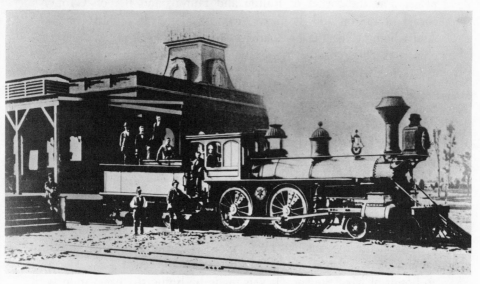

Mr. Stewart's steam
locomotive under the
platform shed of the
Garden City station,
and (below)
the station itself.

The new railroad also had a spur to Hempstead, running about one block east of and roughly parallel to the Long Island Rail Road's Hempstead Branch from Mineola. It left the Stewart main line soon after crossing the rival line at "Hempstead Crossing," ran down what is now Magnolia Avenue to Meadow Street, and continued to a Hempstead terminus at Fulton Street. It proved to be a serious rival to the older branch line to that village, and drew heavily on the Hempstead traffic.

The location of this spur was debated for some time. There is a story that Mr. Stewart and Mr. Ebenezer Kellum went to Hempstead to look over likely locations for the terminus. The Sutton Lawrence place, now the corner of Fulton and Hilton, and Bergen Carmen's corner at Fulton and Terrace, were considered, but Harry Sammis' land adjoining the Presbyterian Church at Fulton Street was the final choice as being nearer the business center. After things had been satisfactorily arranged, the portly Mr. Sammis said: "You should live in Hempstead, Mr. Stewart." To which the fragile-looking Mr. Stewart politely replied, "If one may judge from your appearance, it is evidently a healthy place in which to live."

Even before the railroad was finished, the little Village of Garden City (which is now Central Garden City) was beginning to take shape. Roads and the park had been the first concern of Mr. Stewart and his architect, and an excavation had been made on the high ground west of Cherry Valley Avenue for the purpose of obtaining sand and gravel. When enough material had been taken out for the roads and the top soil had been spread over the park, this unsightly depression was later turned into a small lake, called Lake Cornelia in honor of Mrs. Stewart. It was made by lining the excavation with a two-foot layer of clay, cementing up the southern end, and filling it with the excess water (forced out to equalize the pressure in the mains) from a receiving well at its south-west corner. This lake is now Hubbell's Pond, and has been a delightful part of Village life from the beginning.

In 1874, the square four-storied brick and stone Hotel, designed by Mr. Kellum, was built at a cost of $150,000. Standing impressively in the center of the park, it was crowned with a high mansard roof and was further "ornamented with marble, imposing entrances and with spacious piazzas running its entire length." Its 25 rooms were square and high too, but "magnificently furnished" with tapestries, heavy wall mirrors and fine Victorian pieces from the house furnishing department of Mr. Stewart's Great Iron Store.

When the main roads in the Village and around the Hotel park had been laid out, a dozen large Victorian houses were built at about $17,000 apiece, to set the standard of taste and to house the more important and wealthy families of the business world who were supposed to build up the community. Two of these were on Hilton Avenue (the present site of the Hilton Hall Apartments); others were spotted around central Garden City, as far south as First Street and Rockaway Road, where Mr. Kellum used one of them as his temporary office. These large early houses, renting at $1,200 a year, were later called "the Twelve Apostles," and some of them are still standing. Other smaller houses of brick or frame, sometimes called "The Disciples," were built soon after; and all were snugly fenced in and provided with stables or carriage houses.

At this time also, Mr. Stewart built the brick "estate" office, where his agent was to live and supervise the development of the Village. Conveniently near the Hotel, it was located in the park facing Park Avenue, just north-west of the railroad station. Tall and mansard-roofed, it also towered above the small trees, and could not be missed by visitors or clients arriving on the steam trains. Mr. John Kellum died before he could use the building, but his successor, Mr. Hinsdale, moved in as agent in 1874.

Two multiple store units were built between the railroad track and Seventh Street on Hilton Avenue, and their brick frames are still in use. The one nearer the tracks is hardly altered as far as its exterior is concerned; the other, now the Hubbell real estate building, has had a floor added and its facade changed. On Seventh Street itself, a large brick stable for the Hotel was erected. This was later to become the first Village Hall, and was torn down in 1953 after the new Village Hall had been built on Stewart Avenue.

To make it a real "garden" city, the entire village and park were planted with thousands of trees and shrubs, most of which the new railroad carried on flat cars from Prince's Nursery in Flushing. Among them were rare trees imported from Europe, and these are still to be seen surrounding the Hotel and shading the older houses of the Village today.

The "Estate" office (above), and (left) an "Apostle" house and a "Disciple" house, two of the sixty residences built by Mr. Stewart.

Row of stores on Hilton Avenue. One of them was the Village Post Office for many years.

In 1876, the Great Well, the largest on Long Island at that time, was built north of the Hotel where Cherry Valley and Hilton Avenues meet. As *The South Side Signal* of that year expressed it: "Garden City is to have a mammoth well, 45 feet in diameter. Unlimited water supply is the prospect." Sixty years later, in reporting on the well, which "was a wonder and amazement" in those days, *The Nassau Daily Review Star* describes the methods used in building this colossus: "A huge wooden ring was built off Cherry Valley road and workmen started to build a stone wall on top of this wooden ring. After a few courses of stone had been laid, they sent pick and shovel men to work, digging out the sand and gravel inside the ring. By the weight of the stones, the ring sank as the men dug, and as the ring sank, additional stones were placed on top of it at ground level. Eventually the Great Well went down to about 40 feet, although in those days it wasn't necessary to go much further than 14 feet down to get good water."

An event as exciting as the completion of the well called for a celebration. Accordingly a brass band was imported to the little village from New York; residents and five volunteer companies from Hempstead's fire brigades paraded; dinner was served to guests at the Hotel; and Mr. Hinsdale held open house, with plenty of liquid refreshments for the firemen, at his "estate" office.

Next to the Great Well, a brick building called the Garden City

The old Stable, built in 1872 for Hotel and general use, and converted into Garden City's first Village Hall in 1927.

*The Great Well,
built by Mr. Stewart
in 1876, Garden
City's only source
of water for
twenty years.*

Water Works was built to house the Holly pumps which pumped the water directly into the seven miles of mains running through the Village. Besides the pumping machines, there were three 37-horsepower boilers, which furnished the steam for heating purposes. A brick house to the rear of the building housed the three engineers. The Great Well, with its Holly System, lived up to all expectations and was the sole source of water supply for the Village for twenty years. After that, when the more modern battery of wells was sunk, it continued to serve as a storage reservoir for water pumped from artesian shafts, until it was filled in and its superstructure torn down in 1956.

The Gas Works, using the "Maxim process," were built just to the west of the Water Works; and still later a small railroad spur from the Long Island Rail Road's Mineola-Hempstead Branch came in behind the two buildings just north of Eleventh Street to bring in coal and raw materials.

On April 10, 1876, the same year that the Great Well was finished, Mr. Stewart died in his New York home. The funeral, three days later, was an impressive affair. Flags flew at half-mast and crowds lined the streets for two miles to watch the procession of 150 carriages accompanying the coffin to St. Mark's Church on the Bowery.

The estate left by Mr. Stewart was equally impressive and was estimated at over fifty million dollars. Having no children and admitting to no close relatives, Mr. Stewart bequeathed his entire estate to his wife, with the exception of a million dollar legacy to his great friend and counsel Henry Hilton, who was also directed and authorized to liquidate the great mercantile business of A. T. Stewart & Co. as soon as possible. Mrs. Stewart, Henry Hilton and William Libbey, a close business associate, were named as executors.

Only a few days after the will had been probated and published, the newspapers had the further surprising news that Mrs. Stewart had not only given Mr. Hilton her full power-of-attorney to manage her estate, but had also transferred to him the entire business of A. T. Stewart & Co. in consideration of his waiving the million dollar legacy. It was also announced at this time that a new partnership had been formed between William Libbey and Henry Hilton to carry on the business of A. T. Stewart & Co. in spite of Mr. Stewart's last wishes.

That the exchange was fantastically favorable to Henry Hilton cannot be denied. The company, at the time of Mr. Stewart's death, consisted not only of a tremendously successful wholesale and retail business which was later held to be worth $12 million or more, but of numerous mills and real property here and abroad, and also of substantial money assets. According to Mr. Harry E. Resseguie's exhaustive and scholarly study of Stewart's affairs, the assets which Henry Hilton acquired overnight for nothing were worth $25 million at the lowest possible valuation.

Henry Hilton's affiliation with Mr. and Mrs. Stewart's affairs dated back to 1850, when Mr. Stewart chose him from one of the law firms he employed to be his private counsel, secretary and advisor. Twenty years younger than Stewart, Hilton's youth, shrewdness and promise had apparently appealed to the childless and aging millionaire, and he had leaned on him increasingly over the years. The ambitious young lawyer had proved capable and resourceful, had ironed out countless legal and personal problems for Mr. Stewart, had drawn him into exciting and important municipal activities in New York City, and had aided and abetted him in Stewart's larger political ambitions. His marriage to a favorite young cousin of Mrs. Stewart cemented the bond, so that it is not surprising that the elderly and unworldly widow now put her entire trust in him. That he took advantage of this faith became evident later, but for the present Henry Hilton was in control not only of Mrs. Stewart's affairs but also of the Village of Garden City.

4

THE CATHEDRAL

The death of Alexander Stewart came as a great shock to the Township of Hempstead. No provision had been made in the will for the continued development of Garden City; and worried citizens, contractors, village and railroad employees, feared for the future of the enterprise. Would it after all turn out to be "Stewart's Folly," as had been predicted over the past seven years?

Mrs. Stewart, the devoted and loyal widow, made haste to reassure everybody, however, that the founder's plans would be carried out. Two months later she and Judge Hilton had even more important news for those concerned with the village—namely, that she had planned a lasting memorial to her husband by offering to build and endow a Cathedral Church and Episcopal Center in Garden City, with See House, schools and parish buildings to complement it. As the historian Ross later wrote: "Church, schools and bishop's palace were her free offering to the Diocese, and all she asked in return was that the group of buildings should become the Seat of the Bishop of Long Island and that the crypt in the Cathedral be the resting place of her husband."

The project met with strong protest from the clergy, who felt that Brooklyn, the City of Churches, should remain the center of diocesan

Mrs. Alexander
Turney Stewart,
who built and
endowed the
Cathedral and the
Church Schools
as a memorial
to her husband.

The Cathedral under construction, photographed during
the cornerstone-laying ceremony on June 28, 1877.

life. It was reasonably pointed out that the Plains were still a wilderness, Garden City only a half-realized dream, and that the nearest village, Hempstead, already had its own historic Colonial churches.

But the Right Reverend A. N. Littlejohn, D.D., who had been consecrated first Episcopal Bishop of the Diocese of Long Island eight years before, highly approved of the plan and may even have suggested it. Frustrated, up to this time, in his effort to establish a cathedral and suitable diocesan center in Brooklyn, he must have felt that Mrs. Stewart's elaborate and lavish plans for a Garden City memorial church to her husband could solve his problems and give her added satisfaction. When it became evident that she and Judge Hilton were willing to cooperate in this larger scheme, his enthusiasm could no longer be opposed by the clergy. Consent was also readily given by Dr. Moore, rector of St. George's Protestant Episcopal Church in Hempstead and by the vestry of the Parish, under whose jurisdiction Garden City fell. Nothing remained except to clarify the plans and choose an architect.

Interested Garden City residents soon saw surveyors mapping out a 60-acre tract of land south and west of the Hotel and park, to be used as church property. It was reported that the land to the west of the lake was to be used for a large boys' school, and that the high level area between Fifth and Sixth Streets, on what is now Cathedral Avenue, sloping down in the rear to Rockaway Road, had been chosen as the site of the Cathedral. The bishop's palace was to be built south of the church; and land to the east would be available for a deanery and a girls' school.

Panorama of Garden City in 1884, viewed from
Rockaway Road and Third Street, showing

The Cathedral

Soon, too, it was common knowledge that Henry G. Harrison of New York had been retained as architect for the Cathedral. This seemed eminently fitting, since he had an excellent reputation and had already made some plans for the simple community church which Mr. Stewart had expected to build. The contractor-builder was to be Mr. James L'Hommedieu, who had built most of the existing buildings in Garden City. Bishop Littlejohn was of course to advise on ecclesiastical requirements, assisted by the Rev. Dr. Drowne; Mrs. Stewart was to be consulted constantly, and Judge Hilton would naturally assume control of the financial angle.

According to contemporary writers on the subject, severe clashes of personality and opinion occurred. When Judge Hilton first saw the blueprints of the large Gothic cruciform church, he is said to have taken a red crayon and drawn a line through the two transepts of the Cathedral. Bishop, architect and advisors were aghast, but nothing could move Judge Hilton from this decision, even though the outside proportions of the building suffered and the interior seating capacity was reduced "to that of a chapel." Unfortunately, in trying to conciliate all parties, the Rev. Dr. Drowne fell into general disfavor and lost his chance of becoming first Dean of the Cathedral on its completion. Things were complicated even further by the choice of a Mr. E. H. Harris as architect of the See House and of St. Paul's School. Not content with these two buildings, Harris soon involved himself in Cathedral controversies to the great annoyance of Mr. Harrison.

But in spite of dissension and disagreement, the project got under

unfinished Cathedral spire, "Apostle" houses in foreground, and center of Village to right.

way. Over 240 workmen were employed in the building of the church, and by the time the corner stone was laid on June 28, 1877, the walls were 30 feet above ground and a temporary wooden floor had been laid for the occasion. Bishop Littlejohn, with the still-doubting clergy and a "great crowd" in attendance, struck the stone three times with a trowel and blessed it; the *Te Deum* was sung, prayers were offered and the congregation joined in the singing of the stirring hymn "Christ Is Made the Sure Foundation."

As the work on the great church progressed, clergymen and laymen came fom New York, Brooklyn and from all over the Island to watch and wonder. Building a Cathedral in a raw new village with a population of only 550 must have appeared to them a surprising and strange undertaking, and one cannot blame those who wondered if "Stewart's Folly" had not also become Littlejohn's.

Certainly the next few years were to be trying ones. Aside from supporting the memorial project, which was perhaps the least Judge Hilton could do under the circumstances, he seems to have given very little thought to developing the Village itself. Under his trusteeship, it sank into such inactivity and "rural quietude" that a visitor told how he had "stood at the intersection of the main streets and looked all four ways without seeing a man or woman or horse or dog." The Hotel, closed in winter, did hardly any business in summer. The lobby was usually empty; paint was peeling off the neglected verandas, and the few guests, gazing past the struggling saplings and dusty road, watched Garden City's seven commuters come back from New York or Brooklyn on the evening train. Even at the time of the Mineola Fair things were quiet, and as one newspaper implied, no one seemed to know that the village existed: "At such a time," the reporter wrote, "the Mineola Hotel and the various saloons are liberally patronized, but for the traveller, Mineola is more interesting as the junction for Hempstead on the South and Glen Cove on the North."

Mr. Stewart's hope of attracting his employees and others in similar businesses had failed to materialize. Many of the houses stood vacant and the enterprise, according to one historian, "served largely for a year or two to advance the price of Hempstead real estate and to afford land boomers a chance to throw into the market other tracts of the great plain."

To make matters worse, the railroads on Long Island were in serious trouble. The competitive building of roads during the past ten years had overextended the rail facilities on the Island to such a degree that all three systems had gone into virtual bankruptcy. At one stage in 1876 a tripartite agreement had been attempted, with the object of consolidating the three systems into one, but that too had failed. By 1877, all three were in the hands of Colonel Sharp as Receiver.

To effect economies he made several changes, especially in the Garden City area, living at the Hotel as its first "permanent" guest during that time. One was the abandonment of the newly-built Stewart Road between Flushing and Floral Park. The iron bridge over-pass in Floral Park was torn down, and a curve from the Long Island Rail Road's main line was added to form a connection with what was left of the Stewart Road. After this Garden City trains were to run through Jamaica instead of Flushing; and some of them in those days continued out to Bethpage and then on to Babylon over the Central Extension Railroad which had been added soon after the original Stewart Road was completed.

Colonel Sharp also eliminated two of the three stations in Hempstead in 1878, by abandoning the little-used Hempstead and Rockaway Railroad which had been built in 1870 from Valley Stream, and by tearing up the Garden City-Hempstead end of the old Mineola-Hempstead Branch of the Long Island Rail Road. This left only the spur line and station that Mr. Stewart had built from Garden City, to service the Village of Hempstead, and necessitated a certain amount of backing and filling at Hempstead Crossing on the part of trains coming by way of Mineola.

The greatest blow to Garden City fell on November 7, 1878. Along with every other newspaper in the New York area, the morning *New York Sun* had a startling piece of news to relate in connection with the Village:

> This peaceful community, founded by the Merchant Prince, A. T. Stewart, was shocked today to learn that fiends had stolen his lifeless corpse from the church-yard of St. Mark's in the Bowerie, where it had been deposited temporarily. Upon completion of the Cathedral of the Incarnation in Garden City, the remains were to be removed to the crypt, there to rest in eternal peace.
>
> The identity of those who perpetrated this unspeakable deed

35

is unknown to the police and to Judge Henry Hilton. The judge was aroused from his sleep early this morning by George W. Hammill, the sexton of St. Mark's, who told him of the tragic happening. . . . Judge Hilton, who was left a million dollars of Mr. Stewart's $50,000,000, was properly aghast at the crime. He immediately offered a munificent reward of $25,000 for the recovery of the Corpse. This is a fabulous sum indeed.

The crime inevitably became a journalistic feast in all the newspapers. Shovels, lanterns, ropes, bits of newspaper, cuff buttons and a silver coffin plate played their parts as clues. Cartoons depicting the righteously angry ghost of Mr. Stewart pointing the finger of shame at Judge Hilton, surrounded with money bags and haggling over paying guards to protect the grave, were popular. The snoopings of bloodhounds were described in detail; and witnesses with the unlikely names of Skiddy and Garnsby were minutely interviewed.

To the relief of everyone, the building of the Cathedral was continued. The Gothic windows were framed; workmen's tents continued to flank the unfinished structure, and the railroad unloaded further supplies of Belleville stone at the crossing on Cathedral Avenue.

Two years later, despite rumors to the contrary, Judge Hilton announced that he had paid the ransom and recovered the remains of Mr. Stewart. The body, according to popular report, had been returned to New York from Canada on a flat car with a shipment of marble for the Cathedral. Another version of the recovery of the body was later given out by New York's Chief of Police, George W. Walling, who rather vaguely described a secret meeting for that purpose on a lonely Westchester road, between the kidnapper and a young relative of Mrs. Stewart.

Subsequently, still according to legend and rumor, a coffin was brought to Garden City in the dead of night and placed in a temporary vault in the Cathedral by a masked group of men—the only witness being the sexton, who was also night watchman. A few years later, when the Cathedral was finished, the body was transferred once more to the elaborate crypt under the chancel. "And rumor says," according to *The Sentinel*, "that if anyone should touch, unbidden, the vault which holds the bones of the merchant millionaire, a hidden spring would shake the chime of clustered bells in the tower and send an instant alarm throughout the place." Whether the body in this

36

"safe and permanent resting place" is really that of Mr. Stewart, remains one of Long Island's unsolved mysteries.

The steady work on the Cathedral, See House and St. Paul's School, meanwhile, was slowly effecting some wholesome changes in Garden City's fortunes. By 1882 a few new families and permanent residents had been attracted to the Village, and some of the clergy were already moving in. Both St. Paul's School and St. Mary's, founded in 1877, were carrying on in temporary quarters in a number of houses in the Village; and the large 300-foot-long E-shaped building of the boys' school, built of red brick from the Stewart Farmingdale plant, was all but completed, its tall clock tower dominating the landscape. Finishing touches were being made on the 32-room Bishop's palace and within the year Bishop Littlejohn took up his residence. St. Paul's, finished in 1883, provided a chapel where church services were held for two years until the completion of the Cathedral.

The school, with only a few changes and additions, stands on Stewart Avenue as it was built—old-fashioned now, but considered an outstanding building in those days. Although it was a Diocesan School under the control of the Cathedral Chapter, it was run as a military school for the first ten years, the boys wearing uniforms and being drilled on the playground or in their basement "armory" by a U. S. Army Officer. Located in a Cathedral town and possessing a fine new building, the school was to flourish and rank high in sports and studies, but for the time being only a few of the 200 beds were occupied. Clippings of the period show, however, that these boys, along with the day students, took an active part in Church and Village affairs. Many of them sang with the boys' choir that came out from Brooklyn on Sundays; others edited a small news sheet called "The Chevron"; many, watching the men hoisting the stone for the Cathedral, volunteered to help by pulling on the ropes; and all appeared at chapel for Morning Prayer, to the delight of St. Mary's students, dressed in their "handsome two-toned blue uniforms, . . . the brass buttons bearing the arms of the Diocese." Unfortunately, the boys once became so unruly on parade that they were marched "in full uniform, band playing and colors flying, right through the mud and water of the lake."

St. Mary's School for girls had to wait ten years longer for its permanent building. But it too was to enjoy a popularity among the residents of Garden City, Hempstead and Brooklyn. Academies and private schools were a necessity in those days for high school education and for adequate preparation for college, the common or public schools being still in their infancy, especially in rural areas. Garden City itself, with a small one-room school above the corner store on Hilton Avenue, could offer instruction only in the first few grades.

Besides the growth of church activities, other events worked toward the development of the Village. In the early 1880's Long Island was becoming recognized as the logical summer playground for wealthy New Yorkers. Beaches near New York, such as Manhattan Beach, Rockaway and Long Beach, were blossoming with large hotels, and handsome estates were beginning to dot the north and south shores as well. Further inland the "hunting crowd" were buying large tracts of land for their houses, stables and clubs, especially on the edges of the Great Plain. August Belmont, Jr., Col. William Jay, and Belmont Purdy were among those who located near the village of Hempstead, and in 1881 rented an extensive tract of land from the Stewart Estate for their Meadow Brook Hunt Club. The land ran from Fulton Street in Hempstead to Old Country Road south of Carle Place and Westbury, and embraced the area now occupied by Mitchel Field, Roosevelt Raceway, and the Meadow Brook Parkway. Besides Meadow Brook Club, Mr. Belmont also organized the Hempstead Farm and Kennel Club. As a result, a wealthy group of residents and summer people were attracted to Hempstead and Westbury and some to Garden City as well, where houses were rented for the "season," and the spruced-up Hotel developed a modest summer business.

The Long Island Rail Road was also flourishing by this time. Austin Corbin, a wealthy and experienced man, had bought the bankrupt line in 1880, replacing Colonel Sharp. He was to be president for 16 years, and almost immediately he began the changes which were to turn a rundown, overextended and badly equipped railroad into a road well organized and efficiently run. Long Island and all its villages and towns were to profit by the changes—Garden City, just beginning its career as a suburban and Cathedral village, in particular. Under the new regime, local trains ran regularly and efficiently from terminals in Brooklyn, encouraging commuters and churchgoers; through trains could be flagged for connections with Bethpage, Baby-

Cornerstone-laying of St. Paul's, June 18, 1879,
Bishop Littlejohn officiating, and Judge Hilton, Mrs. Stewart,
and her brother John P. Clinch, in the foreground.

Artillery practice at St. Paul's
during its years as a military school, 1883-1893.

lon, Patchogue and Sag Harbor; and connections with Mineola and Hempstead were greatly improved.

The crowning event of the period was the completion of the Cathedral of the Incarnation and its dedication on June 2, 1885. On that day, the thousands who came to the impressive ceremony saw the finished church dominating the small Victorian Village and the empty Plains in all its Decorated Gothic grandeur. Looking up at the slender cross-topped spire, they must have found it easy to believe the recent stories of sailors who declared that they could easily see it on clear days from the rigging of their ships as they coasted along the shore to and from the port of New York. They must have found it easy, too, to be satisfied and impressed with the richness of the building, with the variety of carved stone and precious marble, with the superb organ and with the beautiful glass windows imported from England. Although a few were to criticize it as a "candy box church," the general reaction was not only favorable but enthusiastic. Garden City itself probably felt that a new era had begun. It was now a Cathedral Town.

5

THE GARDEN CITY COMPANY

Its role as a Cathedral Town did not, however, prevent Garden City from going through a new cycle of difficult years. Four months after the dedication ceremony, Mrs. Stewart died on October 17, 1886, in her eighty-first year, and was buried three days later in the crypt of the new Cathedral. Once more future plans for the Village were in doubt, and this time for the Cathedral Corporation as well.

Mrs. Stewart's estate had become more involved and complicated since her husband's death ten years before, partly because of the expenses and commitments in connection with the Memorial Church and Schools, and partly because of a series of claims which had been made against the estate by alleged or genuine relatives of the deceased merchant.

Now, soon after Mrs. Stewart's death, still further claims were instituted and old ones revived. These, although tedious, could be dealt with, but it was Mrs. Stewart's own will which, six months later, was to be the cause of a much more difficult and dramatic series of legal battles. These were to last three years, and during that time the Cathedral Corporation, which had already been laboring under an insufficient yearly endowment, had to wait for its promised permanent one; and the Village of Garden City, equally unfortunate, had to drift along under the unpopular management of Mr. Cunliff and the parsimonious control of Henry Hilton.

Under the terms of the will, approximately $2,500,000 had been left in legacies or annuities to Mrs. Stewart's close relatives. The rest of the estate, estimated at ten times that amount, had been left in trust to her nephew Charles J. Clinch and to Henry Hilton, both of whom were also to act as executors. Since Mr. Clinch had almost immediately given Hilton his power-of-attorney and gone back to Paris, the terms of the will had virtually given Henry Hilton entire control of and authority over most of Mrs. Stewart's estate. This included the vast parcels of real estate, money investments, hotels and theatres in New York City and elsewhere, as well as the Cathedral properties, the Village of Garden City, and the Plains to the east.

Inevitably Mrs. Stewart's heirs, to say nothing of the hard-pressed Cathedral chapter, now rebelled against this limitless trusteeship and decided to combine forces to fight Hilton's control and to achieve a partition of the estate. In early 1887 three different suits, charging fraud, deceit, mismanagement and undue influence, were filed against Mr. Hilton by the heirs, and in one suit also by the Cathedral Trustees. The three-year battle which followed was a legal classic, involving some of the most famous lawyers of the time, taxing the resources and patience of everyone concerned, and finally ending in a settlement out of court in 1890.

The settlement and partition of the estate left Henry Hilton a very rich man still. His continued possession of the A. T. Stewart business was certified, and he was allotted the Globe Theatre and other parcels of real estate in New York City as well as a generous amount of bank stock. But although he was allowed to remain executor of the estate, his trusteeship was legally ended and with it his control of the rest of the estate and of the Village of Garden City and the Cathedral Corporation, which now received its promised endowment of $800,000, full possession of its eighty acres of church land, and the promise of a new building for St. Mary's School. From this time on Mr. Hilton seems to have dropped out of Garden City and Cathedral affairs, and it is doubtful if he ever visited the Village again. The rest of his life was spent in dissipating his great wealth through unwise management of his great mercantile business (eventually bought by John Wana-

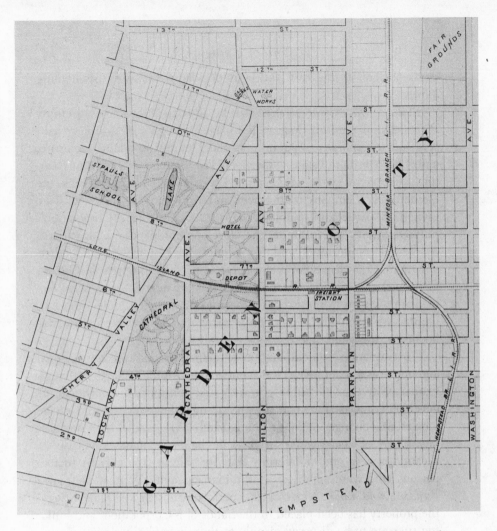

*The Village, with its 60 houses, hotel, church buildings and
railroad, as taken over by the Garden City Company in 1893.*

maker), in fighting continuing law suits and in eventual retirement to
his large Saratoga estate.

The settlement and partition of the estate assigned the remainder
of Mrs. Stewart's estate to her heirs, who subsequently liquidated
large portions of it and made plans to consolidate what remained. This
was of the greatest importance to the future of Garden City, because
instead of dividing and breaking up the "Stewart Purchase" on Long
Island or allowing promotors to get hold of the Village and the thou-

sands of acres to the east, the heirs decided to manage this holding jointly.

It took a few years to arrange, but by 1893 the 5,000 acres of empty Plains east of Clinton Road to Bethpage were divided into large parcels and incorporated separately as the Hempstead Plains Company and The Merillon Estate respectively. In January of the same year, the 2,600 acres west of Clinton Road were incorporated as the Garden City Company by the heirs and a few close friends who were invited to participate. Capitalized at $2,500,000, the Corporation's purposes were "to continue the development of the Village as a residential community," and "to acquire, hold, sell, lease and otherwise manage or dispose of real estate and personal property in Queens County, Long Island." Headquarters for the new business were immediately set up in the old "estate" building near the Hotel, and Mr. Cunliff was temporarily retained as manager. A New York office was opened at the same time.

The formation of a corporation with these wider and less personal aims came as a relief to everyone connected with the Village. Although Garden City was still to be governed and controlled by outsiders, its development was now assured, and along lines which would create wholesome changes. Almost immediately Mr. and Mrs. Stewart's firm policy of keeping the property in their own hands gave way to a cautious new one of offering land for sale at $10 a front foot to persons who were approved by the management. As an item from a *Building and Loan News* of the period expressed it: "The title to the property has been placed in the hands of a Corporation, and building sites are to be disposed of only to those who really desire to erect cottages, in order to keep the town out of the hands of speculators."

Apparently it was high time for this step. Newspaper articles had quite frankly been referring to the Village as "a failure," and had blamed that condition on the fact that the land had never been for sale and that the houses could only be rented. According to Mr. George L. Hubbell, who moved to Garden City with Mrs. Hubbell in 1891, the place was "long on land and short on residents"; streets of empty lots stood forlornly surrounded with broken-down fence pickets, jokingly called "Stewart's ribs" by visitors; and many of the 60 houses were still unrented when the Hubbells arrived in town.

Now, under the new regime, the young couple won the approval of Mr. Cunliff, and pioneered in 1893 in buying land on First Street and Cathedral Avenue. That same year Mr. Baldwin and Mr. Cowl bought and built nearby, and others eventually followed suit in other parts of the Village.

Mr. Hubbell's move to Garden City was connected with the Long Island Rail Road's plans for a new branch line which was to run southwest from the Village. Having worked for the railroad in various departments, Mr. Hubbell was now purchasing agent, and in that capacity was to procure the right-of-way for the new line and to implement its construction.

Accordingly, in 1892, The New York Bay Extension Railroad was incorporated to build a cross-Island branch from Hempstead Crossing in Garden City to Valley Stream, from which point it was to skirt Jamaica Bay, join the Bay Ridge division of the Manhattan Beach Railway, and run to the water front. Its object was to connect with the existing branch to the north between Mineola and Oyster Bay, and to develop passenger and freight traffic across the Island, and also to New England and New Jersey by means of ferry connections.

President Corbin's ambitious hopes for the inter-state connections of his railroad were never realized, but with Mr. Hubbell in charge, the new line was built from Garden City as far as Valley Stream. Finished in 1893, it was operated by the Long Island Rail Road as Lessee, and became a useful cross-County line, and even served as a bi-weekly excursion route between Oyster Bay and Far Rockaway in the summer. It was important to Garden City in the nineties in that it linked the Village with those to the north and south as well as to the east and west. For the expanding Village of Hempstead, the new railroad was even more welcome in that it provided a station in nearby West Hempstead. (It is no longer in use in Garden City, but still operates from West Hempstead to Valley Stream.)

That same year, the Stewart heirs conveyed the fee of Mr. Stewart's Central Railroad Company, from Floral Park to Bethpage, to the Long Island Rail Road, which had been operating it since 1876—thus consolidating the holdings of the line in the Garden City area.

In spite of the new railroad, Garden City was anything but popular in the Township of Hempstead in 1893. The older villages looked down on the new one, which twenty-three years before had sprung into being on the empty Plains at the whim of a millionaire. They instinctively resented the fact that outside money had built the town, the two railroads, the Cathedral, the Church Schools, the biggest well and the widest streets. They found it hard to understand the "outsiders," the heirs, who now owned the Village and the outlying Plains, but did not even live in the Village. As *The New York World* of July 28, 1893 expressed it: "There is a growing element in Hempstead that has always looked askance at Garden City. It is felt that it is too much of the kid-glove community to suit the ways of a homespun town."

But the greatest resentment was caused by the assessment question which involved Garden City and Mr. Cunliff, who represented the heirs through the Garden City Company. During that year, Queens County Supervisors had fixed the 1893 taxes for the townships and had increased them considerably to meet the State Board's demands. In equalizing the taxes between the townships, the Supervisors had added half a million dollars to those of the Township of Hempstead (which included Hempstead Village and Garden City), over and above its pro rata share, bringing the rate to $1.64. This increase related to the assessed valuation placed upon the "Stewart Purchase," which, according to the Supervisors, had been too low for years.

Actually, the assessment had been ridiculously low ever since Mr. Stewart had purchased the land in 1869 for $55 an acre. Being unimproved land at the time, the entire purchase had been assessed by Hempstead Town Assessors at the minimum rate. By 1892, in spite of immediate and subsequent improvements, it was still being assessed throughout at $25 an acre. In 1893, the Board of Assessors timidly raised the assessment to $42, which was still far too low to meet the Supervisors' additional increase for the Township.

Mr. Cunliff, quite naturally, had used whatever influence he could muster over the years to keep the rates at a low level; and when he heard of the Board's action he immediately filed a protest against the new assessment, claiming it to be excessive. This put the Township in an unhappy situation. If Mr. Cunliff were to succeed in his protest, the Township as a whole would have to bear the burden.

Inevitably, indignation and hard feeling against Garden City, the heirs, Mr. Cunliff, and the local assessors, burst out in press and pulpit, or wherever two or three people gathered together. Feeling was to run even higher when Supervisor Edward Townsend made a political football of the matter. Besides being a County Supervisor, elected on the Democratic ticket, Mr. Townsend controlled *The Oyster Bay Pilot* and *The Jamaica Standard*. Through these papers he started his campaign against the Garden City Company and the Republican Mr. Cunliff, calling himself "the man who dares to fling the gauntlet at the feet of the heirs of A. T. Stewart." His battle cry was "No discrimination. Treat rich and poor alike. . . . Why should the hardworking farmer be taxed more in proportion than the millionaire speculators?" In April 1893, *The Pilot* wrote: "A very important question will be decided in the Town of Hempstead this year at the elections, whether the farmers and small taxpayers will continue to bear more than their just share of the burden of government, or whether land which owners are holding at 2 to 5 thousand dollars an acre, should be assessed at $25 or $30 an acre. I refer of course to the Garden City Company. The people are getting tired of nonresident landlords and are asking why this corporation is unduly favored. . . . The people of the Town of Hempstead have carried the Garden City property along for nothing about long enough. Besides this, the Cathedral with its worshiping machinery cost more than $2,000,000 and St. Paul's School and plant a million at least, . . . and they are all exempt from taxation." A few days later *The Pilot* went even further when it wrote: "One of the Assessors last year was a paid employee of the Stewart heirs, so two and two can easily be put together. The thing the Company can do is to secure a manager of their property who will let politics alone."

Mr. Cunliff stood firm, however, and the application of the Garden City Company for a writ of certiorari to review the assessment was served and later referred to the Supreme Court in Brooklyn. The case was further complicated by the heirs and two or three other shareholders who demanded that the Stewart properties east and west of Clinton Road be assessed separately, and not lumped together. Eventually the matter was cleared up; separate assessments were made; assessed valuations were raised from $365,625 in 1892 to $480,500 in 1895, and in 1896 the Town of Hempstead received from the Garden City Company and the heirs of Mrs. Stewart, back taxes for the years 1893-4-5 totalling $17,206.07. The Town, however, had to pay the cost of litigation and counsel fees.

6

THE GAY AND GOOD NINETIES

The Directors of the Garden City Company had by this time realized that their role as absentee landlords was not a satisfactory one for the proper development of the Village. As worldly and successful men, they also realized that Garden City was worth cultivating, not only as an investment but as a project in which they could take pride. Newspaper clippings of the next few years indicate that they increasingly devoted time and energy to the Village. The names of Prescott Hall Butler, Charles J. Clinch, Judge Horace Russell, Stanford White, James Clinch Smith, Frank Sayre Osborne, Devereux Emmet, Maxwell E. Butler, Jabish Holmes, Jr., and Allen W. Evarts soon became well known in civic and social affairs.

A case in point was Judge Russell's wise handling of the first decision which Garden City had to make in 1893, in regard to applying restrictions to the sale of property within Village limits for purposes other than home building. The managers of the Queens County Agricultural Society had offered to buy the 25 acres of land between the Fair Grounds and the railroad tracks for the purpose of enlarging their County Fair activities. Judge Russell, representing the Garden

City Company, set a price of $10,000 on the property and farsightedly laid down restrictions which were to set a zoning pattern of protection for the Village for many years to come. In this case, the land was to be used "primarily for the purpose of a fair and exhibit ground in connection with the present grounds of the Society." Secondly, in the event of the Society ceasing to use the premises, they could not be used "for any factory, shop, hotel, livery or boarding stable, lodging or tenement, boarding or apartment house, hospital or institution; and . . . no building . . . should be erected thereon except private dwellings." After a good deal of complaint the sale went through with only slight modifications of the restrictions, and the Mineola Fair Grounds were subsequently enlarged, fenced in and improved. New brick exhibition buildings replaced the old wooden structures and tents of the past; the half-mile race track was regraded, and new horse sheds and a larger grandstand constructed. The September County Fairs held there were bigger and better than ever, and lasted until 1953, when the property had to be absorbed by Nassau County for governmental purposes.

This sale was followed in 1894 by that of the Meadow Brook Hunt Club to its members, who had leased the large tract of land between

*Mineola Fair Grounds, Washington Avenue and Old Country Road,
in 1890; Mineola-Hempstead Branch train at the right;
Central Railroad train, Cathedral and Village, in right background.*

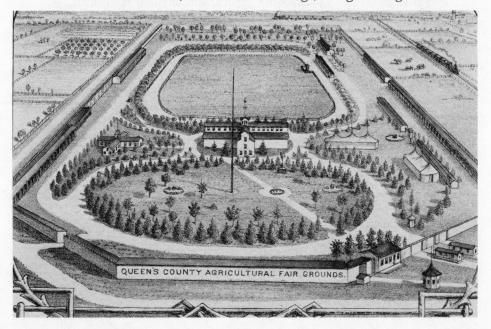

QUEEN'S COUNTY AGRICULTURAL FAIR GROUNDS.

Westbury and Hempstead from the Stewart Estate for the last fourteen years. During these years the club had become one of the outstanding hunt clubs on the Island and was at this time developing a
polo team. Made up of an exclusive and wealthy membership, the
club provided a good deal of social life as well as sport to the area.
Meets often started at the Mineola Fair Grounds, and the open
meadows south of the Fair Grounds to Stewart Avenue were regularly used as a supplementary practice polo field. A number of polo
ponies were kept at the Hotel stables, and members used the Hotel
for hunt breakfasts and dinner parties. After the purchase of the
property, plans were immediately made for a new Meadow Brook
club house, larger stables, a golf course and new polo fields. Within
a few years these plans had been carried out, and the famous Meadow
Brook polo matches were drawing enthusiastic crowds from near
and far.

With this excellent example in mind, the Garden City Company
decided to improve the local Garden City Club, a modest organization
consisting of a small club house and two grass tennis courts located in
the park diagonally across from the Cathedral. Built ten years before
as the "Stewart Arms," its original purpose had been to cater to out-
of-town churchgoers as a place to rest, meet friends, wait for the
steam trains, or water the horses. Villagers had found it a convenient
gathering place too, and as the years passed, had gradually enlarged
its functions to include croquet, tennis, and amateur theatricals.

Encouraged by the Garden City Company's offer to give the members the exclusive use of the old club house and several thousand
dollars to make improvements, the club lost no time in reorganizing
itself as the Garden City Casino Association, open to all residents of
the Village. Plans for extensive remodeling of the building were soon
made, and were subsequently carried out with such dispatch that by
April 17, 1895, the governors of the new club were able to welcome
residents, their guests and the Directors of the Company to a formal
opening celebration. According to *The Herald*, "The spacious ball
room was handsomely decorated and an orchestra of ten pieces
furnished the music. Dancing began at half-past ten, and at midnight
supper was served."

The Casino club house is basically the building we know today, except that in 1895 it was new, had a smoking and billiard room, rocking

chairs on the porches, and a 30-foot portable stage with scenery and curtains painted by the scene designer Baron Rosenkrantz, who was staying at the Hotel. It also had a well-staffed dining room and grill where luncheons and dinners could be served. As one of the few sources of entertainment in the Village, it was immediately popular. Although still primarily a tennis club, it also offered bowling and billiards, and the ladies saw to it that there were weekly concerts and theatricals, "soiree musicales," daily afternoon teas, euchre and debating clubs, lectures, dances, and cotillions. Mr. August Porrier was the manager, and also did a very brisk business in bicycles as agent for the Columbia Bicycle Company.

That same year the Garden City Company took its greatest step toward developing the Village, when it contracted for the remodeling of the old Hotel. Through Stanford White, husband of one of the heirs, the prominent New York firm of McKim, Mead and White was chosen to design the new building. It was planned to house 200 guests, and its purpose was to make a bid for the growing stream of New Yorkers who were coming to Long Island for sport and recreation. According to the less enthusiastic *Recorder,* however, the heirs entered the hotel business "as a sort of fad and last expiring effort to boom and build up the pet scheme of the deceased merchant prince."

This "last expiring effort," nevertheless, proved to be very successful; and combined with the new policy of selling land, the rebuilding of the Casino, the building of the Carteret Gun Club, the bicycle craze, and the development of a nine-hole golf course, it suddenly

The Hotel as remodeled in 1895 by McKim, Mead & White.
It was gutted by fire four years later, in September 1899.

launched Garden City into its first real prosperity and popularity. Newspaper clippings of the middle and late nineties make it evident that the years were really "gay" and good ones for the Village.

The new Hotel was of course the focal point of most of this welcome social life. Unlike the tasteless, colossal wooden structures being built at this time, it was a dignified four-storied Georgian brick building very like the present one except in size. The central section, incorporating the old eighty-foot-square hotel, was augmented by large wings on either side, bringing the length to 210 feet. As a dividend, "a prettily designed cupola" crowned the central portion; and broad piazzas, which could be glass-enclosed in winter, ran across the front and rear. There were 100 rooms for guests, ten private bathrooms, a large children's playroom on the third floor, billiard and smoking rooms, and a buffet bar in the basement for the gentlemen. An Otis elevator was installed to carry the guests to the upper floors; steam heat and fireplaces were provided to warm them in winter, and elaborate gas fixtures were chosen to insure a flattering light at night. The furnishings upstairs included heavy carpeting, iron bedsteads, oak furniture and lace curtains. But in the first-floor reading rooms and parlors, cherry and mahogany pieces, including a $1,300 rosewood square piano, provided an elegance in keeping with the handsomely embossed wallpapers, the oil paintings and the collection of fifteen Charles Dana Gibson drawings that had been acquired "at an outlay of many thousands of dollars." In fact, the remodeling of the Hotel came to about $150,000, but soon proved a sound investment in spite of the modest American-plan rates of "$3.50 a day and up" and "$20 a week and up."

The grand opening came on November 16, 1895. It started modestly in the afternoon with open house and tea "presided over by the fair and graceful ladies of Garden City." But in the evening, for a specially invited group, the management provided a program consisting of a vaudeville entertainment by Japanese acrobats, Hindoo jugglers, and a ragamuffin quartette, followed by supper and dancing.

Three nights later, the ladies of the Meadow Brook Hunt Club celebrated the opening with a subscription dance and cotillion. According to *The Inquirer,* "the dance was preceded in the afternoon by a cross-country run by the members of the club. The start was made from the Queens County Fair grounds and more huntsmen were in

Members of the Meadow Brook Hunt Club,
with the ladies riding side-saddle,
assembling in front of the old Garden City Hotel
before an October cross-country run.

the saddle than at any previous run of the season. After the kill the party returned to the hotel for dinner. In honor of the occasion, the hotel was handsomely trimmed with laurel, fern and chrysanthemums, and a full orchestra, behind a screen of ferns, furnished music. . . . Only the smart set participated."

With such a send-off, the popularity of the Hotel was assured, especially as the manager, Mr. M. F. Meehan, trained in the New York Park Avenue Hotel, ran the establishment in a style to satisfy the most exacting guests. He soon followed the opening events with special luncheons, recitals, lectures, balls, sleigh-rides and dances, and saw to it that such tempting dishes as Sweetbreads-Toulouse, Stuffed Lobster-Cardinal, Roast Gosling, Compote of Squab, Almond Soufflé, and Charlotte Russe-Clamart, were on the menu. Whiskies, liqueurs, and vintage wines of all sorts were also available to diners, as were Mineral Waters or Punch Lalla Rookh for the more abstemious.

Guest lists of the next few years reflect the quality of the clientele which the new hotel was attracting. These lists are studded with such distinguished and glamorous names as the Bordman Harrimans, the Pierpont Morgans, the Astors, the Cushings, William K. Vanderbilt, Jr., Mrs. Peter Cooper Hewitt, Charles F. Havemeyer, the Belmonts, the Ladenburgs, the Jays, Lillian Russell, and Mrs. Burke-Roche. This lady seems to have been one of the reigning beauties of the day, according to the many social clippings which refer to her comings and goings, and which describe her personal appearance. The socially-minded *Sentinel* enthusiastically reported in the spring of 1896 that "while driving the other day, Mrs. Burke-Roche wore a remarkable gown of navy blue which fitted her as if she had been melted and poured into it. The high bodice opened over a vest of chiffon, which greeted, with a graceful caress, a striking collar of lace over pale green silk. . . . The hat to this costume was made of white braided straw covered with a mass of corn flowers, and two large American Beauty roses nestled affectionately just over the coil of her luxuriant hair."

Costumes such as these, perhaps with a light veil and duster added, were worn by popular and wealthy hotel guests as they drove about Garden City in handsome carriages, runabouts, phaetons, or even Tally-ho and "four-in-hand" coaches. The Tally-ho and four-in-hand were undoubtedly "the proper thing." Nearly every pleasant afternoon at five these handsome turnouts could be seen on the Garden City roads, and several times a week coaching parties from Edgemere, Flushing and Far Rockaway made runs to have lunch at the Garden City Hotel. In fact, the Edgemere coach, *Good Times,* with Auriel Batonyi as whip, broke the record run between the two villages in the spring of '96, covering the fifteen miles in 59 minutes.

Those who were not driving about had fallen under the spell of the bicycle craze, which was then at its height. Men, women and children, fashionable or unfashionable, individually or in bicycle clubs, rode wheels, tandems, or imported tricycles. Saturdays and Sundays saw Garden City invaded by hundreds of bicycle enthusiasts from out of town. Clutching "Cyclist's Paradise" maps, they arrived from New York and Brooklyn by the Long Island Rail Road, which provided specially-designed cars "for carrying the bicycles safely." Garden City was their natural rallying-point, objective, or point of departure, with lunch or dinner at the new Hotel as part of the expedition. According to *The Inquirer,* a group of seventy men from the Knickerbocker Athletic Club of Brooklyn made the run one Sunday to work up an appetite, and the next week seventy-five members of the 23rd Regiment of the National Guard rode out for dinner. In fact, the general exodus on Sundays, according to *The Sun* of May 14, 1896, caused the Church Club of Brooklyn to consider the feasibility of a portable "bicycle church, which was to be used solely as a worshipping place for wheelmen." And since "the true wheelman is always seeking new fields and might not like to ride over the same roads every Sunday," it was to be a light frame structure that could be moved from place to place during the summer, at convenient distances from Brooklyn. There were of course to be "suitable sheds constructed in which the bicycles could be left during the service," and no effort was to be spared to make the church accessible by means of good roads and bicycle paths. As the clergy so wisely put it, "If the church wants the bicycle riders it must meet them halfway."

According to the same article, "the Garden City Cathedral would have many cyclists within its doors on Sunday were it not for the wretched roads from Brooklyn." These sandy and dusty roads, however, did not keep local enthusiasts from riding all over Garden City, both Sundays and weekdays, or from investing in the latest models, at $35 to $150 or more, which Mr. Porrier of the Casino, and his rival Thomas Allen, had in stock. In fact, *The Sentinel* reported that nearly all the prominent society ladies who lived or summered in Garden City were riding about in "pretty and bewitching costumes," especially Mrs. Burke-Roche, whose grey and white costume blended well with her silver-mounted wheel. A few local cycle clubs were soon formed in the Village; and the Casino, which complained that wheeling had prevented tennis matches from being arranged, organized a May bicycle parade instead, consisting of a tour through the town and a short run to Lynbrook and back again. By 1897 the craze had reached conservative St. Paul's School. It was announced that the School would build a quarter-mile bicycle track at the cost of $1,000.

Two other sports, meanwhile, were quietly gaining in popularity both in Garden City and all over the Island. Gun clubs, popular for many years, were now demanding more elaborate equipment; and golf clubs, dedicated to that fascinating and irritating game recently introduced from Scotland, were springing up in all sports-minded communities.

Garden City had organized a small gun club in 1894 under the leadership of Mr. Nicoll Floyd, Jr. and Mr. Dudley B. Fuller. Its charter members soon built a small wooden club house east of the Great Well, and had the building, grounds and traps wired with electricity for clay-bird shooting. *The Brooklyn Eagle* of June 1895 reports that the interior of the little club was nicely arranged "and the walls hung with suitable portraits and paintings, each of which is framed with spent cartridges, fired by various members of the club on these grounds." Practice shoots were held on holidays; but all the members looked forward especially to the serious inter-club Saturday matches which were run off for prizes and sweepstakes.

But by 1897 this modest setup was out of date. When the Carteret Gun Club of New Jersey offered to combine with the Garden City Club "for the purpose of laying out a pigeon-shooting plant that would eclipse in extent and perfection of arrangement anything hithertofore attempted," the offer was accepted. In April of that year, after a gay dinner at Delmonico's in New York, members of both clubs worked out the merger. A ten-year lease for property in Garden City was soon obtained from the Garden City Company; and the new building and installations, designed by Richard Howland Hunt, were begun soon after. The site chosen was approximately where Carteret Place is today.

The building was a one-story octagonal affair with a "snug lounge for ladies" in one wing and a gun room in the other. The main lounge room, with a small bar attached, had huge double plate-glass windows, through which the observers could see both shooters and traps. Kennels, coops, and keepers' sheds were provided also, and a nine-foot fence, painted an "atmospheric color," surrounded the grounds. Even before the opening in October 1897, shoots were started, to compete for the $1,000 collection of cups which had been donated, and for the prizes, amounting to $3,000, which the club had appropriated for the season's shooting. Regular shoots, necessitating shipments of 1,300 birds for each day's sport, were soon taking place on Wednesdays and Saturdays; the grounds proved to be among the fastest in America; special trains were run to bring enthusiastic members and guests from New York and Brooklyn, and the Garden City Hotel was busier than ever.

Unfortunately, the fence proved too low to keep wounded birds within the grounds. By 1898 the residents of Garden City were up in arms against the new Carteret Gun Club. "They claim," said *The*

The Carteret Gun Club with its nine-foot fence and installations for live-pigeon shooting; and (foreground) the Island Golf Links with sheds at left for the 200 sheep used to keep it in condition. Gas and Water Works, upper right.

New York Times, "that the firing of guns and the slaughter of birds is a public nuisance and should be abolished. Several home owners report that after every shoot dead or wounded pigeons are found on their grounds or porches." The clergy were not slow to take up the cause, and before long it was rumored that "the club which had moved to its present headquarters during the previous spring and prepared the grounds at great expense, would very likely have to seek new quarters once more." Within a few years these rumors became fact, the club being moved to open country east of the Village.

Golf proved to be a happier choice. In the early nineties Cedarhurst, Shinnecock, Oyster Bay, St. James and Meadow Brook had already established courses; and Garden City, with a new and popular hotel, now felt the need of following the fashion. Accordingly in 1896 a small enthusiastic committee was formed, consisting of Mr. Hubbell and Devereux Emmet, representing the Garden City Company, Dr. Gamage, headmaster of St. Paul's, and Alexander Finlay, who was called in for his professional opinion. After visiting other clubs and studying available areas in the Village, they chose the open Plains lying north of the lake and west of the new Gun Club to Old Country Road—an ideal site, suitable for an excellent all-year-round course. The ground was found to be soft and friable, little affected by frost, and covered with a tough sod of red-top grass "such as is found on the links in Scotland." There were also natural sand and water hazards, and enough variety in contour, caused by the glacial outwash channel running through the area, to make the grounds interesting.

A nine-hole course with a playing distance of about 3,000 yards was accordingly mapped out, and an appropriation of $1,500 requested for its construction, with an additional $1,000 for maintenance during the first year. In spite of some opposition on the part of certain members of the Garden City Company, the request was granted and the project begun. Fairways were roughly cleared of blackberry vines and hummocks, and vigorously rolled with a heavy horse-drawn roller. The greens, leveled off with carpenter's adzes, were swept with stable brooms, fertilized, seeded, and watered. Two hundred or more sheep, bought and put under the charge of the greenskeeper, were herded over the fenced-in course and housed in sheds attached to the pale-blue wooden fence of the Gun Club. An old farmhouse near the ninth tee was converted into a small club house, and other dressing- and locker-rooms were fitted out in the Hotel. The cost of building these first nine holes came to $1,791.82, and another $1,500 was spent on the club house and in fencing the course. In spite of running over the budget, it was with a feeling of triumph that the reception committee sent out invitations for the formal opening on May 29, 1897, of The Island Golf Links—a subscription course built and maintained by the Garden City Company, and open to all residents, their guests, and patrons of the Hotel. Season tickets were priced at $10; the charge for players who wished to experiment with the game was 50¢ a day; the same charge was made for lessons of one hour, and caddies ran to 15¢ for a game. Mr. Porrier, never behind the times, promptly opened a sporting-goods shop in the Village to supply golf-sticks, balls, and suitable attire; so it is not surprising that over one hundred residents, as well as a large group of students at the Cathedral School of St. Paul, had joined before the opening. A group from the Meadow Brook Club were also present for the ceremonies, which included a round of golf for thirty-eight players, with luncheon for all at the Hotel.

The course lived up to all expectations. As *The Commercial Advertiser* of June 1, 1897, wrote: "It is one of the finest courses in the country, extending a mile and one half over rolling prairie country. . . . Each green is connected with water from the city water works, and two hundred and fifty sheep are herded over the course to keep the grass nibbled short and the sod in perfect condition. The links are proprietary, but it is proposed to form, among the annual subscribers, a club which will become a member of the United States Golf Association, thus securing the right to compete in all tournaments."

Although the sheep were soon given up because of their excessive zeal in nibbling a weed called "killcalf," the Club prospered and became so popular that by the following November plans were in hand for enlarging it to a full eighteen holes. These new plans called for an ingenious use of the grounds to provide for the unusually long playing distance of 6,245 yards, which Mr. Emmet advised. But this was satisfactorily worked out, and in due course players were struggling over "sporty and vexatious" holes with such names as The Lake, The Valley, The Prairie, and The Bottomless Pit.

A year later, due to the success of the enlarged course, The Island Golf Links was reorganized, and on May 17, 1899, incorporated as

The Garden City Golf Club, absorbing those members of the earlier club who wished to be affiliated. Women members of the earlier club, however, could join only as associate members, the excuse being that the course was "too vigorous for ladies." Very few availed themselves of this doubtful privilege, and soon even these dropped out.

The new club soon joined the Metropolitan Golf Association, which held its first Amateur Championship Tournament on the Garden City links that year. Two others were held on the course later; and three Amateur Championships of the United States Golf Association were also on the agenda. Moving in such exalted circles called for a new and adequate club house. Ground, east of the lake, had already been broken for a modest building also designed by Richard Howland Hunt, but new plans were now drawn and the foundations enlarged for a building in scale with the larger plans of the club. The building cost $14,196, but was destined to be altered and enlarged once more into the club house still in use today.

The reorganization and high-powered plans of the Garden City Golf Club probably led to the formation in 1899 of a small informal neighborhood club in the southern part of the Village, called The Midland Golf Club. Composed of forty-five members, women as well as men, it laid out its nine-hole course on open land between Franklin and Hilton Avenues south of Fourth Street, an area which the Garden City Company allowed the club to use without rent or taxes. Posts and wooden fences were removed from the site, mowing machines and rakes requisitioned, shallow sand traps installed, and a small club house, once an annex of St. Mary's, erected near the first tee on Fourth Street and Hilton Avenue. In spite of the fact that the membership had to maintain the course and club house, dues were only $6 a year, which somehow managed to cover tournaments, prizes and a rousing 4th of July baseball game with refreshments as well.

With all this enthusiasm for the new game seething in the Village, it is not surprising to read in *The Sentinel* that "Golf links have been laid out on the grounds adjoining the See house. Rev. and Mrs. W. P. Bird and friends find much enjoyment in the contests almost daily engaged. It is not improbable that the Bishop will soon follow suit."

7

THE EVENTFUL NINETIES

Aside from these gay social doings, more serious activities were also being carried on in Garden City during the nineties. Bishop Littlejohn may have joined his daughter in playing golf on their lawn, but his great interest lay in developing the late Mrs. Stewart's plans for further diocesan building. Under his guidance, St. Mary's south wing was erected in 1892 on Cathedral Avenue, and in 1896 the Cathedral Corporation went on to build the deanery to the north of the school, and the electric power house on Cherry Valley Avenue next to the railroad. This plant not only supplied all the church buildings with light, but, by means of tunnels fanning out from its lower regions, also provided them with piped steam heat. When the plant was torn down in 1946, these tunnels were sealed, but there have been continuing rumors and legends among St. Paul's students about exciting adventures in these subterranean passages.

The building program was of first importance, but the Bishop was equally busy with meetings, annual conventions and with the general expansion of the Episcopal Diocese on Long Island. As new parishes sprang up, these conventions, always held at Garden City, became larger and more important. In 1897 as many as three hundred

61

clergymen assembled at the Cathedral and later "partook of a tempting luncheon at the Hotel." Bloodgood Cutter, self-styled Long Island Farmer Poet, somehow managed to attend this particular gathering. His description of it, in doggerel verse, was published by the Flushing *Long Island News.* It reads in part:

> Here the conventions daily meet,
> Here they each other kindly greet,
> Here they propose, and plans suggest;
> Then they adopt what they think best.

Photographing the convening clergy apparently formed an important part of the program, for the poem continues by saying that they

> With pleasant chat, with pleasing smile
> Front of Cathedral stood awhile.
> The photographer in front was seen
> A getting ready his machine. . . .
>
> The Bishop did in center stand
> With noble clergy on each hand.
> Silent and steady we all stood
> So each one could be taken good.

Another gratifying aspect of the Chapter's activities was the growing success of St. Paul's School. With an enrollment of over 120 students, it was becoming not only scholastically well thought of, but was making quite a reputation for itself in sports, playing all the outstanding teams in the New Jersey, Brooklyn and Connecticut areas, and winning a good part of the time. Newark Academy could shout "Hokey, pokey, sock the ball, Here's the time we do St. Paul," but to no avail. Even Lawrenceville, strongest preparatory school at the time, lost the baseball game, 3 to 2, to the Garden City boys in 1896. The victory was such an event that, according to *The Sentinel*, "the whole school met the victorious team at the arrival of the 10:50 train and hauled them up to the school in a farm wagon, with fireworks, brass band and other noisy accompaniments."

A growing and flourishing Cathedral Chapter, a remodeled hotel and three new clubs were things to take pride in, but Garden City could also boast of extended telephone service in the nineties. In 1896 the New York & New Jersey Telephone Company completed its trunk system on Long Island, made Hempstead one of its central offices, and inspired *The Inquirer* to rise to new reporting heights: "Where the 'woach ho' of the savage was heard throughout the domain of the uncivilized Montauks two hundred years ago, and the signal fires blazed forth the tidings of victory and defeat, today from one end of Long Island to the other is heard the gentle 'hello' of the telephone operator."

Subscriptions took a great jump, of course. In 1882 there had been only 800 subscribers on Long Island (Garden City had one telephone in 1885), but by 1896, on the completion of the line, there were 6,000, with the number growing at a rate of 100 subscribers a month. Many of these were Garden City residents and business people; and soon the 'gentle hello' was heard in the Casino, Mr. Rushmore's drug store, Mr. Akley's butcher shop, and probably in Mr. Grodzki's barber emporium.

Another change in Garden City's fortunes came on January 1, 1897, when Mr. Hubbell became general manager of the Garden City Company upon Mr. Cunliff's retirement. Mr. Hubbell had been living in the Village for six years by this time; had implemented the building of the railroad to Valley Stream; had built the first privately-owned house in Garden City, and, with Mrs. Hubbell, had been active in civic, church and social affairs.

At the death, in 1896, of his friend and employer, Austin Corbin, President of the Long Island Rail Road, Mr. Hubbell decided that he would leave the railroad and accept the general managership of the Company. That the job was to keep him busy for the next twenty years was something he could not foresee, but its challenging aspects were enough to attract him. Garden City had reached that stage in its development when it would either remain a small village dependent on its large fashionable hotel and its renowned Cathedral, or would become a well-rounded first-class community. Its unusual paternalistic organization, as a community completely owned and operated by a corporation, called for a manager who fully understood the situation, could see the problems disinterestedly, and could cope with them from the viewpoint of both resident and agent. According to clippings from newspapers of that year, Mr. Hubbell was considered a happy choice. As one rhymster put it:

> When our new agent gets to work
> He'll shape things right side out;
> He's much to do and much to mend
> And much to learn about;
> But he's the right man for the place,
> Of that we have no doubt.

It didn't take Mr. Hubbell long to make a start. Because of the popularity of the gun and golf clubs, he persuaded the Garden City Company to call in McKim, Mead & White once more to finish off the third floor of the Hotel for additional guest space, and the attics for servant quarters. He enlarged the livery and boarding stables on Seventh Street, built a ramp to the upper level, and added new surreys, runabouts and phaetons for the use of patrons.

Village affairs received prompt attention also. To begin with, all the workmen of the Company were given a much-needed pay increase of 25 per cent. This included the staff of forty men running the large farm which had been operated on the fringes of the Village ever since Mr. Stewart's time. When frost left the ground, a new well, the second of Garden City's present battery of wells, was dug on Eleventh Street to insure an immediate safe supply of water until the "Great Old Well" could be cleaned and the slag from the gas works removed from its vicinity. Before long the gas works themselves were banished to an area south of the Village. After building two new ice houses and checking on all public buildings, the energetic manager turned his attention to improving roads and streets, and began working for the macadamizing of Franklin Avenue.

Perhaps his most far-reaching contribution was the pressure he brought to bear on the Company to place Village land on the market at reasonable prices and with more reasonable restrictions, and to provide every inducement for prospective purchasers to choose Garden City as a place to live. To this end he had the broken-down "Stewart's Ribs" removed, the lots cleared and made presentable, markers installed and new fences built for those who bought lots, and prices carefully graded according to location. Families renting houses were encouraged to buy; but in any case, the Company houses were put in proper shape, and repairs and maintenance were stepped up. Plans for new and up-to-date houses were also made, temptingly circulated and advertised. To provide funds for all these expensive improvements, Mr. Hubbell persuaded the Garden City Company to take out a mortgage of $250,000, all of which was to be spent on the improvement of the Village.

The same liberal policy was extended to the Plains east of Garden City and the Meadow Brook Club. On February 4, 1897, this notice was circulated:

> Farm lands to rent, 100 acres or more at $6.00 per acre. . . .
> With buildings, 30 acres or more at $10.00 an acre; or on a five
> year lease for 50 acres or more, a barn, truck house, shed and
> corn-crib will be built at the rate of $10 an acre.

Farther east, the Stewart brickyard at Farmingdale, under the direction of the new management, discontinued its line of common red brick and began experimenting with and producing new types of dry pressed bricks in various colors. This necessitated the latest improved machinery and the newest methods, but proved a great success and increased business immensely.

Nearer home once more, Mr. Hubbell prevailed upon the Long Island Rail Road to replace the old-fashioned high-platformed station with a long, low brick building, complete with a "suitably covered driveway, where passengers could enter carriages without being exposed to rain and storms." By May, 1898, work had been started on the station, which is still in use today. It was built a little to the west of the old one, "to allow for an unobstructed view of the park from the Hotel." According to the faithful *Sentinel*, it was planned to be the finest station on the road, and its completion would provide "yet another example of what push and enterprise always does; and the Manager, Mr. Hubbell, is entitled to the credit."

Garden City affairs were naturally important to Mr. Hubbell and to the Village, but outside affairs and responsibilities were beginning to demand attention as well. Residents and commuters who watched the new station being built were also aware that the Long Island Rail Road was working on a large yard, just east of Garden City, for Camp Black, principal recruiting station for the Department of the East; that three sets of barracks were already in use on the Plains; and that volunteers were streaming through the camp on their way to fight in the Spanish-American War.

The Plains had been used for the billeting and drilling of troops in the Revolution, the War of 1812, and the Civil War. Now, in 1898, they were being used again; and this time Garden City, newly built on the Plains, was inevitably being drawn into the drama and tension of the event. In spite of the new well, Hempstead was chosen to supply water for the Camp, but Garden City's post office was pressed into service. Residents did what they could for the transient troops, and the Hotel, "far enough inland to avoid stray shots from Spanish warships," had never, according to *The Sentinel*, "been so full of prominent guests at one time—members of the Governor's Staff and the officers of the National Guard being registered there."

Even more vital to Garden City than the brief war, was the political excitement and ferment seething in the three eastern townships of Queens County in the late nineties. For many years there had been sporadic but strong agitation for the consolidation of townships adjoining New York City into a Greater New York, and by 1894 the Legislature had passed a law providing for a referendum on the question. In the case of Queens County, the eastern townships of Oyster Bay, Hempstead and North Hempstead had not been included in the bill for consolidation and had been unable to vote. Voting in Queen's western townships had only been half-heartedly in favor, but even so the Legislature had passed the law in 1896.

Now, in 1898, one-third of Queens County automatically became a borough of New York City, leaving the eastern townships in the unhappy position either of seeking consolidation also or of seceding from Queens County and forming a county of their own. Representatives from Oyster Bay, Hempstead and North Hempstead met soon after the New Year at Allen's Hotel in Mineola, and there, after discussing alternative possibilities and actions, unanimously agreed to withdraw from Queens and create a new county "free from entangling alliance with the great city of New York."

Bitter opposition from Democratic quarters in western Queens, and numerous delays in committee, held up the bills which they drafted that winter; but in May, Governor Black finally signed a bill providing for the erection of Nassau County on January 1, 1899.

Garden City, being a small and new village, had no part in any of these events—its only brush with town and county politics having been the unfortunate assessment fight in the early nineties. In fact, up to this time, residents had even found it inconvenient to vote, since every election day meant a trip to Childs' Seed Store in Floral Park. Mr. Hubbell, good Republican that he was, had been working over the years for a separate election district, and in the meantime had consoled himself by organizing "train parties" and "carriage pools" to get the reluctant voter to the polls. With the formation of the new County, he now had hopes not only for a separate district, but for an opportunity to serve the County.

It had been stipulated that the County Seat was to be within one mile of either the Mineola or the Hempstead station, and it was assumed that one of these villages would win the coveted prize. But Mr. Hubbell apparently reasoned that Garden City was equally eligible and might have a more desirable site than either to propose. Soon meetings were being held once more, with the prompt result that Hempstead came forward with an offer of eight acres of farm land near the West Hempstead station. The next week Mineola urged the acceptance of five acres between the railroad tracks and Old Country Road. In May, Mr. Hubbell, with the permission of the Garden City Company, offered "as a free gift to the County" a four-acre site of Company land east of Franklin Avenue between Third and Fifth Streets. The Long Island Rail Road, probably because of Mr. Hubbell's previous affiliation with it, offered to build a station, to be called "Nassau Court House," at Hempstead Crossing, if this site were chosen.

It is interesting to imagine what Garden City would be like today if this site, now that of Doubleday & Co., or if the second proposed site, now that of Franklin Court, had met all requirements. It is probably fortunate that both were rejected as being too far from the specified stations, as were the sites in Hempstead and Mineola for other reasons.

Undaunted by the decision, Mr. Hubbell consulted the Garden City Company as to other possibilities, and was ready to appear at the next meeting with an offer of a third Garden City site—this one a five-acre parcel of land bounded by Franklin Avenue and Old Country Road and well within walking distance of Mineola Station. At a general election in the fall of 1899, the citizens of Nassau County voted to accept this offer. And although from the beginning Mineola was thought of as the County seat, Garden City had the satisfaction of having made a gift to the County, and of knowing that the handsome court house, subsequently built in 1902, was actually within its boundaries.

Garden City needed something to bolster its morale that September. On the 7th of that month a fire, starting in the attics and spreading from floor to floor, gutted the famous Garden City Hotel which had been so handsomely remodeled only four years before.

Early that morning Mr. Hubbell's new telephone rang to tell him that a fire had been discovered in the west wing, and that Garden City's one steam fire engine was on its way from the stables on Seventh Street. Before long, fire departments from Mineola, Hempstead, Floral Park, Westbury and East Williston were on the scene as well, valiantly helping to keep the fire in check while guests of the Hotel were safely evacuated and as many of their belongings as possible were salvaged. Before long, too, Garden City residents, as well as large crowds from neighboring towns, had flocked to the fire, which was spreading rapidly. Volunteers joined the firemen in carrying out furniture, bric-a-brac, paintings, silverware, rugs and china, and others rallied around to pile the rescued articles into heaps on the windward side of the burning Hotel.

The New York Times, recounting the events of that forenoon, described what followed:

> "Attention was then turned to saving the wines and fixtures of the café and wine cellars underneath the east wing. Scores of willing workers assisted in the task, and many helped themselves liberally. . . . Bottles of champagne, whiskey and liqueurs were grabbed as quickly as they were brought from the store rooms, and soon the place was filled with a turbulent throng. Manager Hubbell and some of the hotel employees tried in vain to eject the noisy crowd and a riot seemed imminent. . . . Finally Under Sheriff Henry W. Skinner of Nassau County, who was on the grounds, swore in a number of men and dispersed the crowd."

In mid-morning the cupola fell, and by noon the entire building had been gutted, leaving only a blackened and smoldering brick shell— enough however, according to *The Times,* to be used "as a foundation for a new building which manager Hubbell said would be erected immediately on the site."

By the end of the day the fire had burned itself out, and before another day was over Garden City had begun to clear up the debris. As Mrs. Hubbell wrote a few years later: "Such a mess! Ink and china and everything thrown out of the windows together. . . . So later I had the job of giving away quantities of stuff that could not be used. Chipped china went to St. Giles, and the Casino received the old Copenhagen pattern, nice and thick."

The work of cleaning up the "mess" took many days, and by the time it was done Garden City had resigned itself to the loss of its Hotel, and, with Mr. Hubbell and the Garden City Company, looked forward to the new, fireproof replica which McKim, Mead & White were already designing.

Even better than the hope of rebuilding was the fact that there had been no fatalities during the fire, and that none of the injuries sustained by the firemen had been serious. It was encouraging, too, that the damages, estimated at about $200,000, were adequately covered by insurance. Another comforting although unexpected aspect of the dramatic incident, was that it seemed to have brought Garden City into closer touch with adjoining villages. Firemen and neighbors had come to help, had worked hard and long, had taken risks and performed acts of courage, had been involved in a little trouble along with Garden City residents, and had shared in the shock of seeing the finest hotel in their new County go up in flames.

By December, the nineties were almost over. Garden City had had its share of exciting and gratifying events. It had grown in size and prestige, had faced a shattering material loss, had found its place in the community of villages, and was ready to face the new century.

The Garden City Hotel, rebuilt in 1900 after the fire, achieved a new popularity with the coming of the automobile age.

8

TRAINS, TROLLEYS
AND AUTOMOBILES

During the winter, spring and summer of 1900, the rebuilding of the Garden City Hotel went on, and by fall Mr. Hubbell was combing the field for a suitable manager to take charge of the handsome new brick and marble building. The architects had used the same general plan for the new Hotel, but had scaled it up in size, had added two more wings, and had constructed it in five fireproof sections. Inside, they had provided larger and more open lounges, modernly appointed rooms, many more private baths and, as a crowning touch, a "Roman marble swimming pool with shower and needle baths" in the basement. It was a tempting property, and Mr. Hubbell's choice of J. J. Lannin, one-time head waiter of the Manhattan Beach Hotel, as temporary manager, turned out so well that in 1901 Mr. Lannin leased the Hotel from the Garden City Company and ran it successfully for the next twenty years.

But of greater importance to Garden City and to every other village in the new County was the news, in 1900, that the Pennsylvania Railroad had bought the Long Island Rail Road and would build the long-hoped-for East River Tunnel to New York City. Not only did this promise to bring relief from ferry and bridge bottlenecks to long-suffering commuters, but it also promised a boom in Long Island real estate.

Excitement was still high when fresh news came that two electric trolley companies were battling for the franchise to build a cross-County line through Garden City from Mineola, the County seat, to Hempstead and Freeport, and that other plans for an east-west trolley system were also afoot.

By 1902, the Mineola, Hempstead and Freeport Traction Company, having won the battle, began to build its tracks southward on Franklin Avenue from the Mineola terminal at Old Country Road. There was some worrisome talk that the line would leave Franklin Avenue at Eleventh Street and run down Cherry Valley Avenue and Rockaway Road to West Hempstead, but luckily the route was continued down Franklin Avenue through Garden City.

But just as the line approached Second Street, the trolley company was forced to wage another battle—this time with the Long Island Rail Road, whose West Hempstead tracks crossed the road at this point. The railroad, worried not only by competition from the traction company but also by the additional risk of grade-crossing accidents, refused to grant the line permission to cross its tracks.

To make good its refusal, the railroad immediately went into action and began a series of delaying tactics which lasted for three weeks and which proved an exciting diversion for Garden City and Hempstead citizens. According to Vincent F. Seyfried, an authority on traction history, railroad passenger and handcars were shuttled back and forth over the disputed tracks; arguments raged between superintendents and foremen; crews took sides; steam locomotives, on twelve-hour shifts, blockaded the road; and legal controversies between the rivals and the Railroad Commission made headlines in *The Sentinel.*

The deadlock was finally broken by the Commission in favor of the traction company, and trolley tracks were quickly laid. On May 29th the first through car triumphantly left Johren's Hotel in Mineola, "rolled down Franklin Avenue on the east side of the street, a cloud of dust swirling behind it," defiantly crossed the railroad's various tracks, and swung down Hempstead's Main Street and on to Freeport, where a brass band and salutes from a small cannon heralded its safe arrival.

The new trolley line achieved immediate and continued success.

Inexpensive, convenient and intimate in character, it was soon carrying delighted customers from the villages on its route to the Mineola Fair Grounds in the spring and fall, to the new Court House, to the harbors and beaches of Freeport, and to and from the growing Village of Garden City.

There is no doubt that the line played an important part in developing Garden City and that it definitely earmarked Franklin Avenue as its main thoroughfare. In fact, by 1905 workmen and skilled craftsmen were "riding the cars" to the corner of Fifth street, where St. Joseph's Roman Catholic Church and parish house were being built. And a few years later, Mr. Hubbell and Directors of the Garden City Company were pacing off the northwest corner of Seventh Street for the new-fangled automobile garage they had decided to build.

Automobiles were a fairly common sight in Garden City in the early 1900's, due largely to William K. Vanderbilt, Jr., millionaire industrialist and sportsman, who often came to stay at the Hotel, bringing his latest foreign or domestic car with him. Other devotees of the new sport came too, and before long Stanley Steamers, Panhards, Fiats, Pope Toledos and Renaults were careening around Garden City's dusty streets by day, and were being housed at night in hastily built wooden sheds next to the stables.

Vanderbilt had won the world's speed record in 1902, clocking 76.08 mph in a Mors, and had clinched it two years later with a record 92.80 mph in a Mercedes. He had raced and experimented with foreign and domestic cars here and abroad, only to find that the latter were decidedly inferior. Hoping to force American manufacturers to improve the domestic product and eager to encourage organized racing here, he persuaded the American Automobile Association in 1904 to hold a race in New York State with himself as sponsor and as donor of the trophy.

Convinced that Long Island was the logical place for the race, Mr. Vanderbilt invited the members of the committee to stay with him as his guests at the Garden City Hotel during the planning session. To judge from results, it was a successful move. Not only was the race to be called the Vanderbilt Cup Race, but the course chosen was a roughly triangular one, encircling Garden City by way of Nassau County roads and turnpikes. Ten laps on this course, the committee decided, would give natives and visitors an opportunity to see the cars and racers, and would bring the total length of the race to the desired 285 miles. October 8, 1904 was the date set for the great event, and invitations were accordingly sent out.

The response from German, French and Italian racers and manufacturers was gratifying, as was that of American contestants. County officials were harder to deal with, but finally gave their permission for specified roads—the Jericho, Bethpage and Hempstead turnpikes as well as necessary cross roads—to be used for the course, provided that the cars be safely piloted by a man on a bicycle through the neutralized sections of Hempstead and Hicksville.

By the end of September, Garden City and nearby villages were full of visitors, cars, racers and mechanics; and the week of practicing which followed provided a fascinating series of minor accidents, breakdowns and emergencies. But on the given day at 5 AM Mr. Vanderbilt climbed into his white Mercedes and left the Garden City Hotel for the packed grandstand in Westbury, where he was to act as starter for the eighteen contestants. From all accounts every sort of mishap occurred that early morning during the attempted starts at two minute intervals: brakes and gears jammed, engines stalled, and competing cars either limped or were pushed to the starting line or left it with a thundering roar. According to one clipping, Mr. Vanderbilt had taken it all calmly, until, "extending his starting salute to the third American [car], he was almost seared by the burst from the protruding exhaust pipe as reddish flames and biting fumes accompanied the departure of the Simplex." In the end only two cars, both French, finished the race; but everyone had had such an exhilarating time that the second Vanderbilt Cup Race was assured.

Not only the second, but the third and fourth Cup races as well, were held on Nassau County roads. But each year, as accidents and tragedies mounted in proportion to larger crowds and increasing speeds, it became more and more evident that this type of road racing could not continue. To solve the problem Mr. Vanderbilt, in 1906, formed the Long Island Motor Parkway, Inc., with himself as president, for the purpose of building a safe, fenced-in automobile toll road through central Long Island with bridges and overpasses spanning all roads and railroad tracks.

Once again Garden City was made the center of operations, while

William K. Vanderbilt, Jr., acting as starter for
the 1908 Vanderbilt Cup Race. George Robertson,
first American winner, in his Locomobile.

Long Island Motor Parkway's toll house
in Garden City, one of twelve identical lodges
designed by John Russell Pope.

the rights of way were bought and arranged for, road beds surveyed, road surfaces experimented with and the twelve toll entrances planned.

The Parkway was to run through the north-eastern corner of Garden City. By 1909, when the section from the Village to Bethpage was finished, Garden City not only had a temporary toll and entrance lodge just east of the bridgecrossing at Clinton Road, but also the main Parkway Office close beside it. Although the permanent toll lodge, charmingly designed in French Provincial style by John Russell Pope, was built soon afterwards, in 1911, the Parkway office had to wait several years for its permanent building. Both are now private residences, and easily recognized.

Road sections from Lakeville Road to Garden City and from Bethpage to Ronkonkoma were all but finished the next year, so that by 1910 the $3,500,000 Long Island Motor Parkway was completed. Races had been held on completed sections during the three previous years, but by 1911 the New York State Legislature abolished road racing of any kind, and subsequent Vanderbilt Cup Races had to be held elsewhere.

The new toll road, however, was by this time coming into its own as a safe and convenient automobile road. Even before its completion, Garden City had had so many automobile enthusiasts that the Garden City Company had built, in 1907, the steel and cement fireproof garage which is still in use on Seventh Street—a building large enough at that time to house eighty cars as well as a repair shop and motor cab service. Since very few people drove their own cars or carriages at this period, the Company also converted one of its old houses opposite the garage into a boarding house for chauffeurs and coachmen.

9

SUBURBAN GROWTH:
GARDEN CITY ESTATES

The building of so large a garage in so small a community was symptomatic of what was happening in Garden City in 1907. Encouraged by nation-wide prosperity and optimism, by transportation development in Nassau County and by the growing popularity of the Village, the Directors of the Garden City Company decided that it was time once more to make substantial investments and to speed its growth.

Although rentals of Company houses were excellent in summer and the Hotel never more popular, the Village was still "long on land and short on residents" and needed additions to that encouraging nucleus of families who had bought land and built houses within the last few years. Besides the Hubbells and Baldwins, Colonel William J. Youngs and his family had moved to Garden City from Oyster Bay in 1902. The Clement Gardiners, DeLands and Nesmiths had joined him in building on Cathedral Avenue, and the Boardmans, Arnolds and Townsends had located on or near Hilton Avenue. Mr. Ralph Peters, elected president of the Long Island Rail Road in 1905, had moved his family to Garden City that year, and following Mr. Chase Mellen's lead had built close to the former site of the Carteret Gun Club overlooking the golf course. The Cathedral, too, had brought new families to the Village, from that of Bishop Frederick Burgess, who succeeded Bishop Littlejohn on the latter's death in 1901, to those of his new appointees in the church and the two schools.

The forty-page promotional booklet which the Garden City Company published in 1907 reflects its efforts to attract new residents, and its accomplishments to that date. Besides building the new garage, the Company had overhauled the water supply system, had modernized the disposal plant which it had built in 1904, had made further strides in placing electric and telephone cables in underground conduits, had established its own electric plant, and had encouraged the building of St. Joseph's Roman Catholic Church by a token sale of land on Franklin Avenue.

One page of the booklet was given over to the one-story brick public school which had been built in 1902 at the end of Seventh Street on Cathedral Avenue. According to Mr. Hubbell, president of the School Board, it was "a model school in every respect," provided room and a competent teaching staff for the first six grades, and had "an unusually good kindergarten."

Most significant of all was the booklet's report on the Salisbury Links, a new golf course which the Directors of the Company had just built and were already successfully operating as a public subscription course. It was an eighteen-hole course of 5,858 yards, resembling in terrain the famous championship Garden City Golf course which lay to the north. Almost as sporting and challenging, it had the advantage of being open to all approved players, women as well as men, and of providing, according to Garden City's famous Walter J. Travis, "a good game for all classes of players from the very top-notcher to the veriest duffer." An attractive club house had also been built—two of its most advertised features being "special rooms with private entrance for the exclusive use of ladies," and provision for "refreshments and simple luncheons at moderate prices."

Newspaper clippings of the period indicate that the Salisbury Club with its social overtones was popular from the beginning, and that it soon built up a solid and interesting membership. Along with its own charter members, it absorbed the members of the Midland Golf Club, who had lost their nine-hole course south of Fourth Street to the real estate plans which the Company had mapped out for that area. A great many Hotel guests, especially those staying for long periods, became members too, and others used the course for occasional play.

Perhaps the most important step which the Garden City Company took in 1906 was to sell the large tract of land just west of Old Garden City to an outside development company. During the last few years, syndicates and land speculators had been trying to buy property all over western Long Island with the hope of making a killing as soon as the new tunnel and subway connections to New York City were finished. The Garden City Company had received several such offers for parcels of Stewart land during that time, and in 1903 had even had an offer of $3,000,000 for the existing Village and the Plains on either side.

But it was not until 1906 that a reputable group, including such well-known names as Gage E. Tarbell and former Lieutenant Governor Timothy Woodruff, made an offer that appealed to the directors. This was for the purchase, for $1,500,000, of the one-square-mile tract of land west of St. Paul's School, stretching from Westminster Road on the east to Tanners Pond Road on the west, its north and south boundaries touching Mineola and West Hempstead respectively. The purpose of the purchase was to develop and operate the area as a separate suburban entity to be called Garden City Estates, and in planning the new community to follow the general pattern set by Mr. Stewart.

The tract was an empty prairie except for the railroad track, two or three dirt roads and a small farm. But by 1907 the Estates Company, employing the services of two skillful landscape and civil engineers, Cyril E. Marshall and Charles Leavitt, Jr., had laid out the projected development along its present lines.

Copying the best features of Old Garden City, the planners mapped out equally wide streets, indicated extensive planting, and suggested desirable lot patterns and park areas. Since Mr. Stewart and his architect had emphasized the station and surrounding park as a distinctive feature of the older community, the planning for the Estates Section included a handsome station set in its own large park.

By early spring, a chunky steam roller and many pieces of horse-drawn road-building equipment were operating in the area chosen for the new railroad station, and before long the stucco-and-brick building, with its brick-paved plaza, had been built on the north side of the tracks. Behind it the park, newly graded and adorned with a long pergola and several rows of sapling trees, stretched to Stewart Avenue. Original park plans had included a community club house, but this unfortunately never materialized. Houses were later built along Stewart Avenue instead, and a small building with two tennis courts on North Avenue, between Kilburn and Brixton Roads, had to serve as a community center.

On the advice of Cyril Marshall, emphasis on the station and park was, however, greatly increased by the construction of Nassau Boulevard as a dual highway with a park-like mall in its center. This idea was so successful that it was copied two years later when Garden City East was laid out, with Stewart Avenue, boasting an even wider mall, as its chief attraction.

The newly-built Nassau Boulevard ran south as far as Cambridge Avenue, where the Estates Company built its only community building in 1908. Stables were going out of fashion at this time, and automobiles were still too few to warrant the building of separate garages. The Company therefore constructed a large rectangular stucco stable-garage south of Kensington Road—appropriately divided inside for carriages and horses on one side and for automobiles on the other.

Mr. Marshall's son, Ernest D. Marshall, who grew up in one of the first houses built in the Estates Section, wrote about these early days for the Thirtieth Anniversary issue of the *Garden City News* in 1953. Touching on the stable-garage, he says: "As residents began to come to our neighborhood, a fire truck was acquired and housed in a small building next to the garage, where a team of horses was available to bring the truck to the scene of the fire. Each member of the Company was provided with a red and green trumpet, three feet long, to use in case of fire. He was expected to open the window and give three long blasts to wake up the other firemen. A huge metal gong with a hammer hung from a tree just south of the Nassau Boulevard Station. My father, a good sleeper, usually learned of the fire the next morning from the grocery man."

According to Mr. Marshall, Nassau Boulevard and the streets around the station area were among the first to be laid out and built, but it was some years before they were properly paved. In the mean-

Nassau Boulevard with its mall,
the station, the plaza and the park.
Note the horse-drawn carriages.

Garden City Estates stable and garage,
also used as a firehouse.

time heavy delivery trucks frequently bogged down in the spring mud, "and in summer the wind blew the dust off the streets in clouds."

Muddy or dusty, all the streets in the Estates Section were given delightful and nostalgic English names. Salisbury and Newmarket were chosen on two counts, since they referred to the area's early Colonial history. Oxford, Cambridge, Eton and Stratford were inevitable choices for other streets and boulevards, while Whitehall, Kensington, Hampton and Wellington proved equally irresistible.

Two early roads originally ran diagonally northward through the Estates Section, one from the west and one from the east. They met at the crossing of the Long Island Rail Road's main line, where Merillon Station is now located, and joined there to form Old Court House Road leading to the old Queens County Court House on Jericho Turnpike. The road running to the northeast was eliminated when Garden City Estates was developed, but the other, branching off from Rockaway Road, was retained and called Merillon Avenue after one of the Stewart heirs.

Stewart Avenue was of course the important road running east-west through the new community. Built as a narrow dirt road thirty years before by Mr. Stewart, it was now greatly widened and the existing planting augmented by a double row of good-sized trees on either side.

It was on this handsome avenue that Mr. Gage Tarbell, president of the Company, built, in 1908, his large stucco house between Nassau Boulevard and Euston Road. Designed by Oswald Hering, popular architect of stucco and concrete houses, it was the largest house in the Estates Section until Mr. Woodruff, vice president of the Company, built his equally extensive clapboard one two streets to the east.

Other attractive houses were soon being framed and completed along Nassau Boulevard and around the station plaza, causing Mrs. Hubbell to remember and write later: "We went away for the summer one year and when we came back, there was Garden City Estates all started. It used to be one of our walks to go up there to study architecture, the houses sprang up so fast."

With the experimental and successful electrification of the Garden City-Hempstead branch of the railroad in 1908, and the opening of the tunnel to New York City in 1910, Garden City Estates grew even faster and began to make a name for itself. To help matters, Mr. Woodruff, who had become president of the Company, sponsored an aviation field that same year in what is now the area north and east of Stratford School.

An earlier field was already a going concern in Old Garden City. In 1909, Mr. Hubbell and the Directors of the Garden City Company had leased the large open tract of land east of Washington Avenue and the Fair Grounds to a group of young would-be flyers of the New York Aeronautic Society. Glenn Hammond Curtiss, pioneer inventor and flyer of airplanes, had just built them a plane, the *Gold Bug,* which had successfully skimmed over their small Morris Park field in the Bronx. At his advice they had come to Long Island that spring to look for "a nice flat place" which would be safer and larger for their more ambitious experimental purposes.

The Washington Avenue field had proved to be a perfect testing ground—so much so that on July 7, 1909, Curtiss had won the *Scientific American* trophy by keeping the *Gold Bug* aloft for a record sustained flight of 25 kilometers (15½ miles).

Preston Bassett, in his *Long Island, Cradle of Aviation,* quotes an account of the flight from the reminiscences of the late Valentine W. Smith: "This airplane looked like an enlarged box kite. The driver's seat projected out in front, and the engine with the propeller, set to push forward, was at the back. It was an ideal morning with no wind stirring, and at sunrise Mr. Curtiss wheeled the machine to the east side of the Fair Grounds, and went up a little higher than the tree tops, and circled around for half an hour. At the end of that time the plane fairly collapsed from the excessive strain, but he had remained in the air long enough to win the prize of $10,000."

A month later Charles F. Willard, a member of the Aeronautic group, had made the first extensive cross-country flight, flying over Mineola and Westbury to make a forced landing in Hicksville. Only a year later the *Country Life in America* trophy had been won by Clifford B. Harmon for his flight from the Washington Avenue field across the Sound to Greenwich, Connecticut. Other young inventors had wheeled their strange new planes out of the big sheds on Old Country Road that same eventful summer to struggle into the air, hoping to prove the success of their new ideas and to challenge or break the records already made. "And on these days," to quote Mr.

83

Glenn Hammond Curtiss in the Gold Bug
over Washington Field, 1909.

The plane was assembled in a large tent
pitched next to the Gold Bug Hotel,
Aeronautic Society headquarters on Old Country Road.

Suburban Growth: Garden City Estates

Bassett again, "Washington Avenue, which was the western boundary of this field, would be lined with motor cars laden with the admiring public. When one of the flyers would bob his plane up and down like a gentle roller coaster, they would all honk their horns in enthusiastic applause."

The Nassau Boulevard field, starting a year later than the Washington Avenue field, became prominent almost at once. Probably due to Mr. Woodruff's influence, it was chosen in 1911 for the week's run of the Second International Air Meet in America. Twenty small hangars were quickly constructed on the edge of the field to hold the visiting airplanes; French, British and American flags bravely fluttered over the new roof tops, and the small grandstand groaned under the weight of eager crowds that came from New York, Brooklyn and all parts of Long Island to watch the fun.

That week, along with the many competitive events, the first U. S. airmail flights were made from the new field to the Mineola Post Office. Earle Ovington, sworn in as pilot No. 1 by Postmaster General

The first Airmail flight,
made by Earle Ovington in U. S. Mail Aeroplane No. 1,
during Second International Air Meet at
Nassau Boulevard Field.

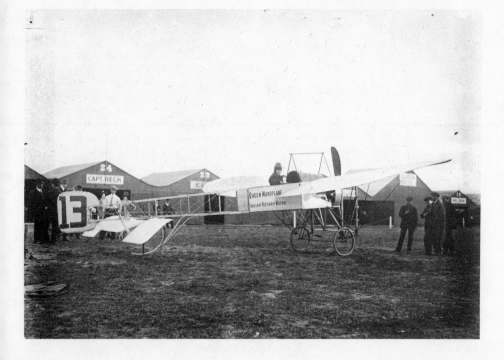

Frank H. Hitchcock, made the several round trips in his Bleriot monoplane, dropping his bags of mail as near the post office as possible and flying safely back each time to receive the applause of the waiting crowd.

A day later Lieut. Milling and Lieut. H. H. Arnold of the Aviation Section of the Signal Corps staged the first U. S. military reconnaissance flights in their Burgess-Wright machines, by flying over the surrounding countryside to locate the several bodies of troops concealed in nearby woods for the occasion.

Flying schools were started at both fields during this period, with Glenn Curtiss heading the Washington Avenue field and Giuseppe Bellanca the Nassau Boulevard field. By 1912, however, as real estate growth pushed northwards, both fields and their schools moved to the newly developed Hempstead Plains Aerodrome east of Clinton Road —a field that was to become famous in aviation history, first as Hazelhurst Field and later as Roosevelt Field. As Mr. Bassett so aptly said of this area, "The airplane had finally discovered its natural home, Hempstead Plains, a friendly ground over which it could strengthen its pinions."

10

SUBURBAN GROWTH:
GARDEN CITY EAST

Airplanes were still "bobbing up and down" over the Washington Avenue Field and the Plains beyond when, in 1910, the Directors of the Garden City Company, encouraged by the success of the Estates Section, decided to enter the field of large-scale development on their own. The obvious direction for such an expansion was to the east of Old Garden City—an area lying within the boundaries of the school district and general limits of the Village.

Garden City East now terminates at Grove Street and its imaginary continuation north through Roosevelt Shopping Center to the intersection of Clinton Road and Old Country Road. But in 1910, the 640-acre "Subdivision East of Franklin Avenue," as it was called on the engineer's maps, extended only to Clinton Road.

Physically, this tract of land was even more an empty prairie than the Estates Section had been three years before. The single railroad track which Mr. Stewart had built in 1873 to link Garden City to Bethpage and the Stewart brickworks ran through it; but the line was largely unused except for an occasional freight or for special trains running to the Meadow Brook Club polo matches.

As for roads, Washington Avenue crossed its western end, running from Hempstead to the Mineola Fair Grounds, and more recently to the airfield. But like Clinton Road, the Subdivision's eastern boundary, it was only a narrow neglected track, muddy in spring and often impassable in winter. The only other road in the empty tract was a segment of the Motor Parkway, which curved through its northeast corner, crossed Clinton Road by means of a concrete and steel bridge, and disappeared from sight as it ran east through the high grass of the Plains to Lake Ronkonkoma.

Probably the only buildings in all this area were the two small temporary structures which Mr. Vanderbilt had built the year before in connection with the Motor Parkway. One housed the toll keeper, and the other was used as an office for Mr. Vanderbilt's superintendent.

It took vision and courage, to say nothing of money, to attempt the transformation of this prairie into a modern suburb. The Directors of the Company had all three requirements, and for experience they turned to Mr. Gage Tarbell, who had proved his ability in developing the Garden City Estates. Leaving his former position as its president to Mr. Woodruff, Mr. Tarbell joined the Garden City Company that winter to help in planning the layout of the Subdivision and to continue as special sales agent under the Company's resident general manager, Mr. Hubbell.

Mr. Tarbell once more engaged Mr. Marshall and Mr. Leavitt as engineers, and with their help and with suggestions from the Directors, worked out a geometric pattern of streets similar to that of Old Garden City and the Estates Section. For relief, a few curved and interwoven roads were added north of Stewart Avenue, with short streets running south of it to the railroad tracks. Since the Directors of the Company were investing a million dollars in the new project, they decided that it was justifiable to name these particular roads after themselves. This accounts for Osborne, Huntington, Wetherill and Lefferts Roads, and for Butler, Clinch, Devereux and Emmet Places. For good measure the two roads paralleling the railroad track were called St. James North and South for the village in which most of the heirs lived. South of the railroad, horticultural names were used exclusively.

The prominent feature of the development was to be Stewart Avenue, bisecting it with its double roadway, its wide mall and six rows of trees. The original plan called for the extension of this 180-foot-wide avenue west to the Garden City Hotel. Houses already built on this street were accordingly moved north to Ninth Street, and some trees were also moved; but the extension was never completed.

The plan also called for a compact brick station at Clinton Road, backed by a semi-circular brick plaza, brick walls and a deep park extending north to Stewart Avenue. The park was to contain a small club house and three tennis courts, as well as winding paths and luxurious planting.

In the spring of 1910 surveyors, road machines, and hundreds of workmen began to carry out the plans for the new project. By the following spring Mr. Tarbell announced that a syndicate had bought one hundred separate lots along Stewart Avenue and Westbury and Osborne Roads, and had agreed to build a group of "high class residences to cost $1,000,000."

Twenty-five large houses, designed by well known New York architects, were actually built that summer, most of them nearer to Old Garden City than to Clinton Road, with the result that the new little station was not used for some years. When development of the

This artist's rendering of Stewart Avenue and the Mall, looking east from the Garden City Hotel, was used in a brochure published by the Garden City Company in 1910.

area justified it, a trolley line was installed to shuttle between the new station and that of Old Garden City.

The following description of this trolley and its route, written by Felix Reifschneider of Hempstead, has luckily been preserved: "Then came the shuttle car. You will recall that the L.I.R.R. built a special track, south of the regular track, which ran about as far as the old freight house built in Mr. Stewart's day between Hilton and Franklin Avenues. There it joined the main track, after making an 'S' curve around the signal post, a curve so sinuous that only the little shuttle car could have made it. The car itself had formerly belonged to the Ocean Electric but had been sent to Huntington, and when it reached Garden City bore the name 'Huntington R. R.' on its letter board. . . . The car was subsequently repainted a sort of chocolate brown, and the 'Huntington R.R.' was painted out, although you could still see it showing through the paint from a certain angle. The car was equipped with third-rail shoes, and the trolley pole removed."

One of Garden City's long-time residents remembers this car too, and that it had a motorman-conductor, old Julius, who conscientiously shuttled back and forth and then settled down to his lace-making frame between trains. A few years later, the trolley ran out as far as Meadow Brook Club and Mr. Lannin's Salisbury Golf Club during the polo and golf season. And during World War I it lent its small services to Camp Mills, Hazelhurst Field and the newly activated Mitchel Field.

One of the important aspects of the development of Garden City East was the Company's decision to promote Franklin Avenue "as a modern business section, to supply the demands of this rapidly growing district." The booklet which Mr. Tarbell got out in 1911 goes on to say: "The restrictions here as well as in the residence section are such as to maintain the character and dignity of the locality. The exterior architecture of all buildings, both residence and business, must be approved by the Garden City Company, and business buildings on Franklin Avenue will be of uniform height."

Franklin Avenue hardly suggested a business district at this time. Looking north from Stewart Avenue there was nothing to see but the single trolley track of the L. I. Traction Company running up to the Court House. To the south, on Seventh Street, the new Garden City Garage loomed as the only sign of the Avenue's future. Beyond, on both sides, a few old houses could be seen; then the main railroad crossing, the Blacksmith Shop sign, a row of small employees' cottages, and beyond these the Roman Catholic Church and parsonage.

But the Garden City Company had immediate plans for Franklin Avenue. In March 1910, a few months after joining the Company, Mr. Tarbell announced that Doubleday, Page & Company, one of the great publishing houses of the country, had bought forty acres of land bordering on Franklin Avenue between Sixth and Second Streets and that a large plant would be built as soon as possible.

Reaction to the news was decidedly mixed—some welcoming the financial relief to the Village, others dreading the possibility of a precedent for other industries in Garden City. Fears were largely laid to rest when plans for the new plant and its extensive gardens were made public and work actually began.

It took only four months to build the all-under-one-roof brick building, designed by the firm of Kirby and Petit "to resemble Hampton Court in England." The structure covered more than six acres and housed not only the printing and power plants, but also the executive

Colonel Theodore Roosevelt laying the
cornerstone of Doubleday Page & Company, July, 1910.

offices, the bindery, carpenter shop, storage and shipping rooms, and the Western Union and telephone systems as well. Theodore Roosevelt laid the corner stone in July of 1910, and by October the Company's seven hundred employees were producing the 6,500 books a day which had been set as the goal.

During those four months the underpass at Chestnut Street was also built, and the Long Island Rail Road cooperated by providing a long platform behind the plant for its new railroad stop, Country Life Press. In 1913, the railroad added the small station which still perches rather precariously behind an even longer platform.

Clearing and grading were started as soon as the building was completed, so that landscape architects could get to work in laying out the elaborate and beautiful gardens which were to surround the plant and continue south along Franklin Avenue to Second Street. Hundreds of well grown trees and carloads of shrubs, bushes, hedging plants and climbing vines were delivered to the site, where trained gardeners placed and planted them according to plan. The results, although not immediate, were more than successful. As one newspaper glowingly wrote: "The rose garden and arbors, the rock garden, the old-fashioned garden, the tennis court, the pool modeled after Falconieri, the famous pool outside Rome, the sundial with its old printer's signs, the front court with its fountains and masses of bloom, surround the plant, so that from any window one can get a glimpse of lovely greenery."

There is no doubt that the completed Country Life Press, as the Doubleday Company christened it, turned out to be a handsome addition to the Village, and that it was responsible for bringing in a delightful group of new residents. It brought a good deal of life to Franklin Avenue too, forcing the Long Island Traction Company to step up its cross-County trolley service and to provide a siding opposite the plant.

Not to be completely outdone in developing the Avenue, the Garden City Company built in 1912 its first business building just north of Stewart Avenue. The lower floor was given over to the Post Office, which up to that time had functioned in one of the small stores on Hilton Avenue; and the upper apartment floors were hopefully listed as being for rent.

The Company also decided to develop the small triangle of land, awkwardly placed between the two branching railroad tracks behind the new Doubleday plant and accessible only from Meadow Street, as a low-cost housing area. "Walk-through" underpasses were built under both tracks to relieve this isolation, and fourteen small Franklin Avenue cottages, displaced by the Doubleday purchase, were moved to the site. A year later the Company built a few stucco semi-attached houses, each with its own brick-walled garden, as part of the area's master plan. Others were added later, and these charming English-style units, complete with bow windows, tucked-in porches and steep-gabled slate roofs, eventually made an appealing group. The development, called Franklin Court, was to go through cycles of popularity and neglect, but was finally to achieve the steady success which has lasted to the present time.

These Court houses and various small houses built by the Doubleday Company, helped to swell the number of residences in Garden City East. Larger houses were also being built throughout the new development, so that by 1916, when Mr. Tarbell resigned as agent, Garden City East had taken its place as a recognized and welcome part of the community.

11

CAMP MILLS:
WORLD WAR I

Sandwiched between the two new developments, Central Garden City inevitably continued to grow and flourish. General prosperity and the electrification of the Hempstead Branch of the railroad brought new families to the older community as well as streams of transients, golfers and other sports-minded guests to the Hotel. Luckily the Garden City Company, although investing heavily in the Eastern Section, did not neglect the original village. In 1911, in cooperation with Mr. J. J. Lannin, the Hotel was greatly enlarged and remodeled once more—this time by the firm of Ford, Butler and Oliver. And in 1912 the Company built five units of double houses on Fifth Street to attract young couples. Two years later it built "Honeymoon Row" on Fourth Street.

Additional construction faced the Company when, in 1911, its office building, dating back to 1873 and Mr. Stewart's era, burned to the ground in the park between the railroad station and the Hotel. Before the debris could be cleared away, a new office (now the Public Library) was being planned for the park, as well as new equipment for the fire house on Seventh Street.

Unfortunately almost all the Stewart Estate and Garden City Company records, maps, surveys and early documents, as well as all the Public School records, were destroyed with the office. These were irreplaceable and their loss has been felt to this day.

Existing school records, as a result, begin with the date May 1, 1911, when the first annual meeting after the fire was held, with Mr. Hubbell presiding. Nothing daunted by having to begin all over again, the Board that year requested and received a budget of $6,000, its largest so far. It raised the principal's salary to $1,000 and teachers' pay to $600, and laid plans for adding a second story to the Cathedral Avenue School to accommodate the School District's 185 children. In the 1912 meeting, $40,000 was voted for the project, two sessions were discussed, and student transportation on the ever-late morning train from Nassau Boulevard was dealt with.

Clubs as well as schools were feeling the pressure of a growing population. The Garden City Golf Club, being a private one, was undisturbed and able to continue its famous career. But the Salisbury Links, built in 1907 as a public subscription course, was so crowded by 1915 that heavy congestion became the rule and players had to arrive at 8:30 on weekend mornings to get a good game.

It was time to make a change, and in May 1916, after receiving permission from the Garden City Company to reorganize as a private club, the Salisbury Links became the Cherry Valley Golf Club, taking its name from Cherry Valley Avenue, which then ran through the course below the club house. Limited to a reasonable and congenial membership, the new club quickly became a popular community center; and, after joining the various golf and tennis associations, it also began to make a name for itself in championship competition.

Former members of the Salisbury Links, living in the fast-growing Estates Section, chose this time to promote a private club of their own. Leasing several adjoining tracts of land west of Nassau Boulevard, they engaged Walter J. Travis to lay out their excellent course, and incorporated themselves as the Garden City Country Club.

When the trend toward private clubs in Garden City became a fact in 1916, Mr. Lannin, lessee and manager of the Garden City Hotel, decided to replace Salisbury Links with a new public subscription course which would bear the same name and carry on the tradition of catering to Hotel guests and other unaffiliated players from New York and Brooklyn. A large rolling section of the Plains

95

east of the Village was already available as a site, since it formed part of his own Lannin Realty Company, which he had been building up over the years through the purchase of small parcels of land in Garden City and of large tracts of the Hempstead Plains. Never one to procrastinate, his plans were soon being carried out, and the new Salisbury Golf Club (now Nassau County's Salisbury Park), just east of fashionable Meadow Brook and connected with Garden City by electric trolley, seemed ideally located.

The timing however was unfortunate. On April 6, 1917, after three years of neutrality, the United States finally declared war, and the impact of subsequent events slowed down and changed all peacetime activities.

In spite of building new golf courses, Garden City residents, like all other Americans, had found the last three years uneasy and frustrating. Shocked by the declaration of war in Europe in 1914, they had eagerly sought ways to help, had joined organizations, sent money abroad, and had, more recently, faced the probability of war for their own country.

There had been constant reminders too in Garden City itself. In 1914, Walter Hines Page of Doubleday's had left his comfortable home on Cathedral Avenue to take up his post as Ambassador to the Court of St. James. In 1915 the New York National Guard had organized an active aviation unit at the Hempstead Plains Airfield. In 1916 the field, renamed Hazelhurst Field, had been taken over as a military post for the training of one of America's first squadrons of flyers. By early summer the squadron's few available airplanes were flying in tidy formation over the Village or attempting maneuvers over the Plains.

Of all of Garden City's residents, Ralph Peters, president of the Long Island Rail Road, had probably been the most actively concerned during this period. Convinced from the first that the United States would become involved in the war, Mr. Peters had turned his full attention to the role which Long Island and its railroad might play in that event.

As early as 1915 he had urged Major General Leonard A. Wood to join him in a track inspection so as to become acquainted with the railroad's facilities and its ability to respond to Army defense plans. A year later the Island had been combed for suitably located tracts of land to serve as camp sites. Track plans to service these sites had been studied, and transportation costs and estimates had been made.

As a result, when war was declared in April, sites in Mastic, Belle Terre, Hicksville and Yaphank had already been examined, and the final choice of the latter site could be made relatively quickly. On July 7, 1917, Camp Upton at Yaphank received its first troop train, composed of a box car, a baggage car, fifteen flat cars loaded with trucks, and one passenger car occupied by seventeen soldiers.

But the building of a permanently appointed cantonment was to take time, and it was not until early 1918 that Camp Upton was finally able to cope with its peak capacity of 35,000 men. In the meantime, a nearer temporary embarkation camp was suddenly needed.

This was for the 42nd or Rainbow Division, which the War Department was assembling from the National Guard regiments of every State in the Union, to be sent overseas as the first of its infantry divisions. Undoubtedly due to the groundwork that Mr. Peters had done, a second site on Long Island was chosen—this time within the very borders of today's Garden City. It was to be called Camp Mills, in honor of the late Brigadier General Albert L. Mills, Chief of the Militia Bureau.

Surprisingly enough, in spite of the recent development of Garden City Estates and Garden City East, there was still just room enough within the general limits of the Village for Camp Mills. The site was the large undeveloped tract of land lying east of Clinton Road, which, since it had belonged to the Hempstead Plains Company, had not been included in Subdivision East in 1910. It was bounded on the north by the Motor Parkway and Hazelhurst Field (later to be called Roosevelt Field). To the south lay Hempstead Village, and to the east the Army's new Aeronautical General Supply Depot, which a year later was to become Mitchel Field.

Chosen for its favorable location and its nearness to New York, its varied rail connections and Garden City's abundant water supply, Camp Mills used all these advantages immediately. Mains were quickly laid in strategic areas, and building material, brought in over Mr. Stewart's Central Railroad, were stored in hastily-built warehouses on what is now Commercial Avenue. Always full of railroad tracks, Garden City now began to bristle with even more, as extra double tracks, sidings, coal trestles, storage tracks, and spurs of every sort were built. The shuttle from Country Life Press station was built at this time too, and served not only through World War I, but World War II as well.

As the days went by, the camp grounds proper were cleared of hummocks, meadow turf and various potato patches, and necessary roads were roughly indicated. It was decided that Locust Street, continued east of Clinton Road, should be the main street of the camp, with smaller roads, leading to supply, parade or tent areas, branching from it.

A paper called *Notes on Camp Mills,* found in the Village archives, contains this short description: "On the left of the entrance from Clinton Road into Locust Street, stood the little wooden Telephone Building, and opposite it on the right was the Information Booth. At first a tent, by a woman's ingenious use of a transported bathing shack, it became a small wooden structure giving protection from wind and rain. Further south on Clinton Road was the 'Visitor's House'—a good sized tent; and slightly east behind it and between them was the Y.M.C.A.'s large tent. Ranging east on either side of Locust Street were the various regimental headquarters, and to the north rows and rows of tents stretched to the railroad tracks."

Only a month after the site of Camp Mills had been chosen, Garden City's first troops arrived. The *Notes,* as they continue, give some idea of the confusion and excitement of that day: "In August 1917, when word came through that the Rainbow Division was arriving, the women connected with the Information Booth and Hostess Houses thought it would be a fine idea to give them iced tea and sandwiches. Tubs of tea and basket upon basket of sandwiches were prepared and ready when the men began to arrive. Tired and thirsty and covered with dust, they fell upon the refreshments—and still they continued to come—more and more of them—13,500 of them, until the distracted women finally attached a hose to a hydrant and the boys sat close along the curb to quench their thirst."

From that day on, residents of Garden City, Mineola, Hempstead and other neighboring towns devoted themselves to improving the lot of the Rainbow Division. Hempstead probably did more for these men than any other, because it was an established town and just down Clinton Road. "Literally thousands of men," according to Felix

Reifschneider, Hempstead's historian, "thronged the streets, . . . sat on the roofs of trolleys and perched on the steps and bumpers, and packed the taxis besides. Every home made the boys welcome and hospitality was unbounded. Eight new restaurants were built and new stores sprang into existence on all sides."

Garden City, still a new village without even a bank, library or public eating place, could do far less. But "every home made the boys welcome" too, and Mr. Lannin held open house at the Garden City Hotel every Sunday evening. The Village's greatest and probably most rewarding efforts were made on Visiting Day. As *The Evening Sun* of Sept. 20, 1917 wrote: "One of the biggest jobs at Camp Mills is the care of visitors. It is estimated that 50,000 people visited the Rainbow Division last Sunday. The whole problem has been taken out of the hands of the military authorities and handed over to a group of women in the area."

By the time the Division went overseas in October, it had become "Garden City's Rainbow Division." Its veterans felt this too, and the monument which they raised after the war to their 2,950 dead and 13,290 wounded, now stands in a small park on Clinton Road south of the railroad station and tracks.

The floorless tents of early Camp Mills were occupied by the Rainbow Division in 1917.

No sooner had the Rainbow Division left than the 41st or Sunset Division moved in. But the weather was much colder by this time, and heavy fall rains had started. It was a windy October too, especially hard on the Y.M.C.A. tent which, "with every hard storm, blew over—until finally it gave up the struggle and settled down in ruins." Under the circumstances the troops, without even flooring under their tents, were continually wet and cold, and soon filled the emergency camp hospital, set up in the Mineola Fair Grounds buildings. By December the camp had to be closed and the troops moved to Camp Merritt.

Except for activities at Hazelhurst Field, Garden City was quiet and deserted that winter, especially as most of its young men and some of its young women had volunteered and left the Village. To fill the void, residents turned their full energies to Liberty Loan Campaigns, the Home Defense League, drives of all sorts, Draft Board Committees and every other kind of war work.

Then in 1918, after the German drive around Cambrai, word came that Camp Mills was to be reactivated in order to speed up the embarkation of troops in the emergency. This time it was to be established as a permanent camp, and once more freight flowed through Garden City into the cantonment, and construction gangs, along with the 42nd Engineers, arrived to cope with it.

In the next few months, better roads were constructed, proper telephone facilities installed, drainage improved by a system of dry wells, and permanent buildings and barracks erected. Mr. Peters' history of "The Long Island Railroad in the War 1917-1919" tabulates facts and figures which give an idea of what Camp Mills was like when completed. To begin with, its capacity, including tent area, was 50,000 men; the number of buildings erected by the Government, 838. Included in the long list of these structures, such items as these occur: 398 Barracks; 36 Officers' Quarters; 108 Lavatories; 1 Liberty Theatre; 7 Post Exchanges; 105 Mess buildings; 1 Laundry; Water and Sewer Pump Stations; 3 Stables; 2 Haysheds; 2 Delousing Plants; 1 Electrical Sub-station; 69 Quarantine Huts; 9 Administration Buildings; and 1 Library.

Facts and figures about Base Hospital No. 2 (2,500 beds) are also given. These reveal that after a check on St. Paul's School and other large buildings in or near Garden City, this new Camp hospital was

*Monument to the
Rainbow Division
on Clinton Road.*

*The formal entrance to the
reactivated Camp Mills of 1918.*

built on Transverse Road, specially constructed as an approach, in what is now the Mott Development. A railroad siding was brought to the empty site for the freighting of necessary materials; and soon after, according to Mr. Peters' history, a spur "from Base Hospital siding, because of using engine as heating plant," was also built.

The hospital, with its unique heating system, was hardly finished before the Armistice of November 1918 was signed, but it served the camp during the following demobilization period and was pronounced a great improvement over the tents, converted stables, cattle sheds and poultry houses of the Mineola Fair Grounds.

Demobilization was to take almost a year. Home troops, still in the United States, were sent to Camp Mills first. Then came "the 814th Pioneer Infantry (colored) just back from Europe and entering camp triumphantly behind the regimental band." Later came other regiments, one after the other, keeping the camp active and crowded.

But by September 1919 the job was almost over. On the 17th of that month, *The Hempstead Inquirer* rather wistfully wrote: "The Meadow Street Canteen on Tuesday evening gave what will probably be the last dance to be given for the soldiers at this favorite resort. There are so few men in camp now that the Canteen will most likely be closed shortly." A week later Camp Mills was officially abandoned and Garden City's great community war experience was over.

Its own young men and women had been coming back too, except for the six men who had died in the service of their country. One, Lieut. William Bradford Turner, had been killed in action on Sept. 27, 1918, while leading an attack against one of the strongest parts of the Hindenburg Line. For bravery on the field of battle, he was posthumously awarded the Congressional Medal of Honor by the United States Government. In Garden City he was honored by its veterans who, in 1919, organized their American Legion Post and called it the William Bradford Turner Post.

12

COMMUNITY AGREEMENT
AND VILLAGE INCORPORATION

Post-war problems were inevitable.
It took the Long Island Rail Road many months to remove the spurs,
sidings, installations and extensive trackage which had made it
possible to move the required freight and over 2,000,000 troops safely
and efficiently to and from Camp Mills.

It took the Government, too, a long time to clear away the buildings and structures on the hospital and camp sites. In fact, foundations and occasional piles of concrete were still being discovered in
the overgrown fields ten years later, when houses began to line the
streets which had once been flanked by tents and barracks.

One tract, however, on Clinton Road between the railroad track
and Stewart Avenue, had been kept clear even while Camp Mills was
being built. This was the land which the Curtiss Aeroplane & Motor
Company had purchased just before the war, and on which in late
1917 it built a large brick plant for the designing and manufacturing
of airplanes.

Its immediate project was to design and build, as a secret Navy
weapon, three large tri-motor seaplanes with power enough to cross
the Atlantic. Although the war was over before the planes were
finished, completed parts were shipped from Garden City in the spring

of 1919 to the Naval Air Base at Rockaway Beach, where they were assembled. In May the flying boats were ready, and although two dropped out because of mechanical trouble, the NC4, after stopping at Newfoundland, reached the Azores and Europe safely. This was a "first" in aviation history.

The plant, later called the Curtiss Engineering Company, continued to develop and manufacture other planes while it operated in Garden City. For its experimental testing it used the runways of Roosevelt Field, and put on a series of flying exhibitions which attracted great crowds from all over the Island and from New York as well.

The Field was now a peace-time field, catering not only to the Curtiss Company, but to aviation schools, flying clubs and barnstorming groups. Always popular, it attracted its largest crowds in 1919 when the British Dirigible R-34, after completing its first flight across the Atlantic, cruised over New York and then moored in the center of the Long Island field. To quote Preston Bassett: "A rigid dirigible was a new sight not only to Long Islanders but to Americans. Thousands of people drove out on the Island to see the huge silver fish slowly swaying at its mooring . . . in Roosevelt Field. At night floodlights illuminated it and the public stayed to admire. It remained there for several days until the weather was right for the return trip, and then one evening it rose, circled New York in a farewell gesture, and was off again to England."

Roosevelt Field, the Glenn Curtiss Company and Mitchel Field, which had been chosen by the Army as the permanent base of the area, were to play an exciting and important role in aviation development over the next ten years. Garden City was inevitably to share in the excitement and wonder of these events, but in 1919 the Village was facing an important step in its own development.

The incorporation of most towns and villages usually follows a reasonable and orderly pattern. But Old Garden City, unique in its paternalistic beginnings, was destined to do it the hard way. Twenty-five years of benevolent and careful ownership, control and management by the Garden City Company had not prepared its citizens to desire or assume responsibility. The newly developed Eastern Section, happy under the same management, felt much the same. If it had not been for the Estates Section, owned and operated by a far less efficient and successful corporation since 1907, things might not have changed for many more years.

But as early as 1912, conditions in the Estates Section had become so unsatisfactory to its residents that they had formed a Property Owners' Association so that they would be able to take concerted action against the management. For a time things improved, but again services became inefficient or even curtailed; promised deed restrictions were ignored, and necessary safeguards neglected.

The last straw came in 1918, when the Garden City Estates Corporation notified the residents that "in the near future it would no longer continue to furnish or pay for the lighting and policing, and the laying out and maintenance of streets and parks."

At this news a small group of residents, with the help of the Property Owners' Association of Garden City Estates, immediately formed a committee to take action. Incorporation of the Estates Section as a square-mile 'Village of Garden City' seemed at first the only solution to its worried residents, but on second thought it appeared hardly fair to Old Garden City, which had prior rights to the name.

A post-war view of part of the famous
Curtiss Engineering Plant on Clinton Road showing (center) a
tandem-wheeled, three-motored "Eagle" and (left) the fusilage of a
"Jenny" with uncovered wing frames beside it. The "F-boat"
(right) had a pusher engine and wing-top stabilizers.

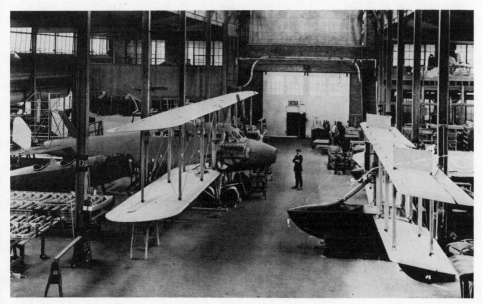

Incorporation along School District lines, embracing all three sections of Garden City as well as the small undeveloped areas lying to the east and west, was the only other legal alternative.

But residents of the older community, although they violently opposed the separate incorporation of the Estates Section, were reluctant to be involved in this wider plan for fear of an additional tax burden and an unfair division of governmental power. This last concern stemmed from the fact that the Estates Section was then growing rapidly enough to indicate that it might soon be able to outvote the combined Central and Eastern Sections.

For the time being, however, things were still on a fairly even keel. With a total population of 2,140, the division of resident property owners and the assessed valuation of each area stood roughly at these figures:

Central Garden City ...... 160 homes; area assessed at $2,340,000
Garden City East .... 50 homes; area assessed at $ 821,000
Garden City Estates .... 160 homes; area assessed at $1,940,000

Considering these figures and faced with the necessity of making some decision, groups of residents from all three sections began to turn toward joint incorporation as the only solution.

One other condition had to be taken into account. This was that the Garden City Company still held roughly 30 percent ownership ($1,794,800) of the real property within the district, and was accordingly in the legal position of having to give its consent to any plan of district-wide action.

Luckily, both the Company and Mr. Hubbell were disinterested enough to favor any plan which would be in the best interests of all concerned. In March 1919, Mr. Allen W. Evarts, its president, expressed the Company's willingness to join the move for School District-wide incorporation.

On the receipt of his written consent, a large meeting of representative property owners was held. Their unanimous decision was to incorporate the entire district, and by April all necessary papers were completed and filed with the Town Supervisor.

Serious trouble still lay ahead, however. Opposition within Central Garden City suddenly flared up once more; petitions were circulated, new threats of separate incorporation were made, and the Garden City

Company, put under severe pressure, withdrew the consent it had given.

It took almost four weeks of debate, committee work, careful planning and endless patience to resolve the problem. But eventually, through the resourcefulness and ingenuity of Mr. C. Walter Randàll, attorney, a "Community Agreement" was drawn up which satisfied all parties.

DECLARATION OF COMMUNITY POLICY

We the undersigned property owners residing in Common School District No. 18 of the Town of Hempstead, being desirous of effecting the incorporation thereof as the Village of Garden City,—and thereafter desiring to assure its future as a village in which the representation of the three main sections, namely Garden City East, Old Garden City and Garden City Estates, shall be and continue to be fairly apportioned;—and also desiring to assure ourselves that the expenses of managing the Village shall be kept within reasonable bounds, without extravagance or unnecessary expansion,—do hereby agree,—each with all of the others, severally and collectively, and each in consideration of the execution thereof by the various others who shall become signatory hereto,—as follows:

1. That the Village shall be governed by a board of four trustees and a Village President, the President and two trustees to be elected annually and the trustees to be divided into two classes of two trustees each, one class to serve for one year and the other class for two years.

2. That the Board of Trustees shall be so maintained that at all times Garden City East shall have one member of the Board of five (composed of President and four Trustees), and Old Garden City and Garden City Estates shall have two members.

3. That the budget for the first year should not exceed the sum of $80,000 and that during that time there is no section of the district which requires any extraordinary expenditures for improvements.

4. That it is the opinion of the signatories hereto that the present scheme of general maintenance of the district should not be enlarged.

5. That each of us shall use his or her best endeavors to

carry out the spirit and letter of the foregoing agreement for a period of not less than five years, or until such earlier time as the number of the property owners of Garden City East shall equal the number of property owners of Old Garden City or Garden City Estates separately.

6. That this agreement may be executed in counterparts, all of which shall be considered together as though the various signatures thereto were contained in but one written document, which shall be filed and kept with the Clerk of the Village.

IN WITNESS WHEREOF, we have executed this agreement in one or more counterparts, all as of the 15th day of May, 1919.

The original declaration now hangs in the Village Hall. It is covered with marginal notes, footnotes, crossed-out sections and additional clauses. It bears witness to the conflicts and tensions inherent in the situation, but also to the democratic method used in solving them.

Careful reading of the Agreement makes it plain that its provisions actually did resolve the basic objections of the opposition, assured fair distribution of elective governmental representation among the three sections, and endorsed a policy of moderation in the village tax burden for at least the first five years of the life of the Village.

Although not a legally binding document, it was signed that evening of May 15th as a "Gentlemen's Agreement" by forty-nine residents representing all three sections of the community. The next morning the Garden City Company once more gave its written consent, and within a short time all legal requirements for incorporation were also attended to. On July 9, 1919, *The Hempstead Inquirer* wrote: "The first election of the Village of Garden City will take place at the Fire House on Seventh Street on the 19th day of July between the hours of 11 AM and 4 PM, for the purpose of electing a village president and trustees."

The election of officers was held in strict accord with the provisions of the Community Agreement. Only one slate was presented to the voters of the Village that day, but the names on this slate represented the choice that each of the three sections of the Village had made earlier through its Property Owners' Association.

When the newly elected officers met for the first Thursday meeting, it was agreed to rotate the presidency year by year during the first five years of the newly incorporated Village. To show its good will, the Estates Section offered to wait until each of the other sections had had the presidency, before taking its turn. Mr. Hubbell, representing Central Garden City, was chosen that evening for this important office. As usual "he was the right man for the job" and was to prove it that first year and the following thirteen, when he served either as trustee or in the role of president (or mayor) during the periods when it was his section's turn to have that honor.

The Village was unusually fortunate in having a man of Mr. Hubbell's experience to start things off. Having served as general manager of the Garden City Company for twenty-three years and also as president of the School Board, he knew the community both as a School District and as a composite of sections each with its own history and special character, and therefore was able to guide it through the transition period as painlessly as possible.

Notices in *The Hempstead Inquirer,* published during the first few months after the legal incorporation of the Village on September 30, 1919, reflect its early problems as well as its unpretentious beginnings. A sampling of them runs as follows:

October 29, 1919: "The Village Board met last Thursday evening at the Fire House. A group of representatives from Stewart Manor came before the board to correct the impression that Stewart Manor wished to withdraw from being part of the incorporated village. Mr. Scott called the board's attention to the bad condition of Stewart Avenue west of Garden City Estates and also the road leading to the station."

"The Board of Assessors reported that it had sat on Oct. 20, Grievance Day, from 9 AM to 1 PM and no kickers had appeared."

"Mr. Naisawald reported that he had purchased furnishings for the village offices and up to the present time had expended $1,513.38. Authority was granted to Mr. Naisawald to have window shades made."

"Counsel Randall was asked to prepare permits and licenses and other applications to be used in village offices."

"Mr. Hubbell was authorized to have the fire truck put in perfect condition to be in readiness for any emergency."

November 12, 1919: "At the meeting of the Village Board a resolution was offered authorizing the treasurer to borrow $5,000 from the Nassau Trust Company to meet various expenditures in connection with the collection of taxes."

"Police Commissioner O'Connor was authorized to purchase overcoats for the policemen, the cost of which not to exceed $54.00."

"Mr. Hubbell reported he had taken up with the Garden City Company the question of securing prices on horses, wagons, etc., which might be of use to the village; that he could secure 8 or 9 teams of horses at $200.00 per horse and wagon. Tools, snow plows etc. could be had at inventory prices."

"The Garden City Company appeared willing that the village should have the use of its stables and grounds in exchange for the payment of taxes and insurance, but that some arrangement be made so that residents could board horses at said stables."

"Mr. Randall had 30 copies of the village ordinances printed and he expected the balance at a later date."

The Code of Ordinances referred to was written by Mr. Randall, printed in 1919 in a small twenty-page booklet, and signed by Theodore B. Klapper, Village Clerk. It covered *Public Peace and Order, Public Morals, Fire Prevention, Licenses, Traffic Regulations* and *Miscellaneous*. It makes nostalgic reading, partly because the problems seem simple in contrast with those of the present day, and because it is full of references to bygone things. License ordinances mention public carts, hack coaches, junk dealers, peddlers, pushcarts, coal scalpers and hawkers. Traffic regulations insist that "all vehicles and horsemen must keep to the right-hand drive" of divided highways. Public Peace and Order rules require that "no horses, cattle, sheep or fowl be allowed at large."

By far the most important ordinance to be adopted by the newly-incorporated Village, however, was the emergency zoning ordinance which the Board of Trustees prepared in 1921 to protect a large area of vacant land in the Estates Section from being sold for unrestricted business and residential use through public auction. This narrow escape luckily led the trustees to appoint a Zoning Commission, composed of representatives from the three sections of the Village, to make a more thorough study of existing conditions and to formulate a set of regulations to control the future development of the Village.

There was little precedent to go by, since zoning for suburban communities was all but unheard of at this time, but by 1924 the Commission had completed its work and the Incorporated Village of Garden City had adopted its first comprehensive Zoning Ordinance. Although there have been subsequent reviews, amendments, and revisions, this basic code is still in use today, and has firmly and far-sightedly provided the pattern of protection which has carried Garden City safely through its tremendous growth. Articles of the Code deal with Residential Districts, Business and Industrial Districts, General Provisions, Enforcements, and Interpretations. It also provides for a Board of Zoning Appeals.

Its early success, as well as that of the Community Agreement, was undoubtedly due to the growing strength of the three Property Owners' Associations. These not only provided the machinery for selecting candidates for Village and School Board offices, but were increasingly called on, over the years, to act in an advisory capacity on budgeting and long-range planning, as well as on zoning.

By 1925, the fourth Property Owners' Association was formed in the extreme western or Stewart Manor section of Garden City, which had now grown large enough to consider breaking away from the Estates Section and seeking representation on the Village Board. This was granted, by Amendment to the Community Agreement on Feb. 2, 1931, when Garden City West was given one member, and Garden City East's representation was raised to two.

Since then no other important amendment to the Community Agreement has been adopted. The four sections have selected their representatives year by year through the machinery of their Property Owners' Associations. One slate of officers, to serve without pay, has been presented to the Village of Garden City each year on election day. Each year the slate has been accepted without opposition. And term by term, the rotation of mayors has been faithfully observed.

The Long Island Press, during several years of reporting on this unusual and non-political form of government, ran headlines which were typical of many other newspapers of the period and which could still be honestly written today: "Garden City settles its political fate by agreement." "Gentlemen dislike fights even in village elections." "Mayor and Trustee will swap positions in Garden City Board." "It all works under a Gentlemen's Agreement."

13

THE TWENTIES

Incorporation of the Village of Garden City had been accomplished and a framework of government agreed upon. Time was to prove that it was a good and workable one, but in the 1920's the Gentlemen's Agreement was to be tested and sorely tried as the new Village went through its greatest period of proportional growth, from a community of 2,420 residents in 1920 to one of 7,180 in 1930.

Although committed to a policy of moderation in spending, the Village trustees soon had to face the fact that drastic steps would be necessary to provide the extra facilities and services which such rapid growth called for. Dependence upon the Garden City Company for rented office space, for water, lighting, sewage disposal, and for the use of garage and stable, was obviously not going to work out indefinitely. The Village would have to buy or build what it needed, and keep house for itself.

The first step was taken in 1921, when the Village bought the old brick stable on Seventh Street from the Garden City Company. Its immediate use was to house the growing police force in the hastily remodeled west wing—the rest of the building to remain as a stable and also as a storage place for maintenance equipment. Long-range plans, which were not realized until 1927, included the remodeling of the entire building into Garden City's first Village Hall. When this was done, the shell of the masonry building was retained, its second floor was finished off, its exterior was coated with stucco, and a small cupola and attractive front portico were added. Since the stable had no cellar, the plumbing and heating pipes had to be "laid on" inside the building as unobtrusively as possible, and other make-shift arrangements for vaults and storage space had to be resorted to. But the general effect, both inside and out, was attractive and dignified—a great improvement on the small rooms over the fire house. The building served for twenty-five years, until the present Village Hall was built in 1953 on Stewart Avenue.

A second purchase was forced on the new Village in 1923, when the three Property Owners' Associations took joint action against the Garden City Company in an effort to prevent an advance in water and sewer rates, and lost their case. Acquiring the two systems was obviously a necessity, and the Village that year assumed a bonded indebtedness of nearly a million dollars to cover their purchase and modernization. The disposal system was brought up to date soon afterwards. The water system, always a source of great pride to Garden City, was able to carry itself as a self-sustaining unit from the first.

Luckily for all concerned, the Nassau Light and Power Company (later absorbed by the Long Island Lighting Company) purchased the electric plant from the Garden City Company that same year, modified rates as a matter of policy, and prevented another source of irritation.

In spite of this reprieve, 1923 proved to be an expensive year for Village taxpayers both on the School and on the Village level. It suddenly became evident that the small brick school house on Cathedral Avenue and Seventh Street, in spite of its two wooden additions, could no longer take care of all the children from the three growing sections of the Village.

Sparked by a canvass of school facilities and a subsequent highly critical report made by two educational experts who had been called in by the women's Community Club, the problem was soon being heatedly attacked in private and public meetings, in Property Owners' Associations and in Garden City's newly established newspaper, *The Garden City News*.

The main issue was whether the taxpayer's money should be spent on one large central or common school or on two extra regional ones. Since this was a regional matter, all the old sectional prejudices, irritations and loyalties, which had made incorporation so difficult, flared up once more. Sections took sides, changed sides, disagreed within themselves and even took steps to split up the School District. Milder warnings came from individuals who could take the situation less emotionally. In a winter issue of *The News,* one taxpayer parodied Lewis Carroll by writing a "Garden City Jabberwocky" which read in part:

> "Beware the Central School my son,
> The fearful tax! The sealing wax!
> Beware the Water-Works and shun
> The small-town verbal wacks."

In the end, after partition of the District had been denied and all sides had been heard over and over again, Garden City's citizens met one December night in a large Village-wide meeting in the Hotel and once more buried their differences. By a big majority, they voted for one central Village school to be built in Central Garden City.

Another inflammatory issue was settled that evening also—namely, the choice of a site for the new school. Two had been available—one the $10,000-an-acre tract of 6½ acres on Cherry Valley Road and Stewart Avenue, owned by the J. J. Lannin Company, and the other a larger tract west of the Cherry Valley Golf Club (now the Adelphi College campus), which was owned by the Garden City Company and offered at $3,000 an acre. The vigorously opposed choice of the more expensive and smaller Lannin property was probably a short-sighted one, but understandable in a day when the population was still under 5,000, automobiles scarce, buses considered dangerous, and the two railroad stations inconveniently remote from the larger site.

In its May meeting, the School Board was authorized to assume a bonded debt of $485,000 for the site and for the Cherry Valley School which was to be built on it. The "fearful tax" proved to be less staggering than was expected, and the handsome school, completed in 1925, not only satisfied the two experts but all the children and parents as well.

Strangely enough, once this first hurdle had been taken, other long-range school plans were soon being considered and implemented. Times were prosperous, the Village was growing faster than ever, the School and Village trustees had proven themselves responsible, and the citizens as a whole surprisingly responsive. In 1925 the purchase of two school buses, dangerous or not, was authorized; in 1927 and 1928 respectively, two additions of eight classrooms each were made to the new school; in 1928 Stratford School was built in the Estates Section; and in 1929 the site for Stewart School in the East was acquired. By the end of the 1920's, firm foundations had been laid for the excellent school system which was to make Garden City famous.

In the meantime, the two Episcopal private schools, St. Mary's and St. Paul's, were doing well. Both were to feel the competition of the improved public school system, especially during and after the depression of 1929. But both schools had earned a solid reputation by this time, and were able to weather both depression and future change.

Besides acquiring a central school, a newspaper, and the ownership of two utility plants, Garden City also acquired a bank of its own in 1923. Mr. Hubbell, with a few associates, founded The Garden City Bank that year and modestly started it on its career in two rooms of his newly remodeled Hubbell Realty Building—one of the old store units on Hilton Avenue. Immediately successful, the new bank was able to build and move to its own quarters on Seventh Street two years later. This building now forms a part of the enlarged and modernized bank of today.

Other private enterprises in the Village in the early twenties consisted of the purchase of the Seventh Street Garage from the Garden City Company, the erection of two apartment houses nearby, and the building of various groups of "contractor" houses in outlying areas. Inoffensive as these smaller houses were, the Village did well to adopt its Building Code and Zoning Ordinance in 1924, so that future expansion could be controlled and regulated. Another new enterprise, launched in 1926 and destined to speed the development of Franklin Avenue, was the new bus service, inaugurated to replace the faltering trolley service of the bankrupt Long Island Traction Company.

All these practical matters, however, concerned only one side of Village life in the twenties; and although they kept Garden City citizens busy and constructively employed, they left plenty of time for social gaiety and for sports. These were wonderful years for making money, playing in golf tournaments, going to races, horseshows and international polo matches, for traveling and for giving parties. Motoring in a "snappy little Saxon," a "Chandler Chummy Roadster" or "Reo Speedwagon" was fun too, especially on the Long Island Motor Parkway, which was so accessible with its handy toll lodge on Clinton Road.

Perhaps the most exciting diversion was watching the Aerial Carnivals at Mitchel Field. In 1923, at a typical meet, the Baring Bomber, largest tri-plane in the world, circled over the field and eastern Garden City, followed by a group of Martin Bombers which flew low behind a quickly laid smoke screen. Later in the show, the large single-engine Fokker airplane, the T-2, famous for its recent transcontinental flight from San Diego to Mitchel Field, swept past the watching crowd; while, lagging behind it, came an old 1910 Curtiss pusher-type plane for laughs.

But more serious projects were usually afoot at the enterprising new Army air base. In 1920, four Army airplanes had taken off from the field for a successful round trip to and from Nome, Alaska. That same year the first Pulitzer Trophy race was won by an Army plane, which left the field to establish a speed record of 156.6 miles an hour. And in 1922, safety devices were worked out for a model cross-country airway between Dayton, Ohio, and the Long Island base.

The Garden City Curtiss Engineering plant on Clinton Road was specializing in pursuit and racing planes during this time. In 1921, a Curtiss Navy Racer won that year's Pulitzer prize; and in 1924 one of its new pursuit planes, built and especially groomed at the plant, set another transcontinental record in a dawn-to-dusk flight from Mitchel Field to San Francisco. A Curtiss racing plane also won the Pulitzer Trophy Race in 1925, by setting a new world's record of 249 miles an hour.

By 1925 Mitchel Field had settled down to orderly flight training and to routine Army life, leaving experimental and spectacular record-breaking flights to nearby Roosevelt Field. It was from this field, during the late twenties, that six dramatic attempts were made to fly the Atlantic Ocean non-stop.

As far back as 1919, Raymond Orteig, a wealthy hotel owner, had posted a prize of $25,000 for the first non-stop flight between Paris and New York. There had been no takers for seven years, but in 1926 Capt. René Fonck, a French war ace, arrived at Roosevelt Field with his Sikorsky biplane and announced his intention of competing. With a crew of three, he made an attempt to lift his heavily-loaded plane from the field one early September morning, only to crash in flames at its eastern end. He escaped, but two of the crew were killed.

In spite of this disaster, Capt. Nungasser and Capt. Coli, also famous war aces, readied their *White Bird* in Paris for an attempted flight in the other direction. Leaving Le Bourget on May 7, 1927, they started across the ocean, but apparently came to grief near the Grand Banks. No trace of the plane or flyers was ever found.

During the same month, Clarence Chamberlin, testing and experimenting with a new Wright-powered Bellanca, *Miss Columbia,* at Roosevelt Field, clocked up a new endurance record of 51 hours and 11 minutes in preparation for his attempt for the prize. During the same period, Commander Byrd, just returned from his successful flight across the North Pole, was conscientiously testing his own large tri-motor airplane, the *America,* for its entrance in the race.

But before Byrd and Chamberlin were ready for their flights, news came that another contestant, a young airmail pilot, Charles A. Lindbergh, was flying east from San Diego in a small new Ryan monoplane named *The Spirit of St. Louis.* He landed at Roosevelt Field on May 12, 1927. The story of this young man's great achievement has been told many times, but the very small part Garden City played in it is worth recalling. The field Lindbergh flew from was located partly within the boundaries of the Village; he spent that difficult week of waiting either at the field or in the Garden City Hotel; his boyish face and tall figure became known to many residents during that time, and many of his younger fans either spent nights at the field in cars or hay wagons, or else came out at daybreak each morning in hopes of seeing his departure.

Preston Bassett wrote of that morning take-off on May 20th: "He was at the field before day-break. It was overcast and still raining, the field soaking wet. The plane was towed to the extreme west end of the field and at 7:52 AM he took off into the gray eastern sky. Somehow the whole setting of the unknown youngster taking off alone with so much confidence and so little show, where war aces and famous

Charles A. Lindbergh with
Clarence Chamberlin on the porch of the
Garden City Hotel, May, 1927.

pilots had failed and where others were still busy with their elaborate preparations, electrified the world."

Lindbergh arrived at Le Bourget Airport after 33 hours and 30 minutes of flying. One of the telegrams he received was from the Garden City Volunteer Fire Department, which he had visited during his week in Garden City, and which now elected him as an honorary life member.

Another young aviator, more closely connected with Garden City's history of the twenties, was Lawrence Sperry, son of Elmer Sperry, inventor of the gyroscope and founder of the Sperry Gyroscope Company. In 1914 young Sperry had won the 50,000 franc prize offered by the French Société Aeronautique for the first stable airplane, when he flew his Curtiss flying boat, equipped with the new gyro-stabilizer, past the judges' stand with his arms over his head and his crewman out on the right wing of the plane. Later, during World War I, he had worked on a secret pilotless "aerial torpedo plane" or primitive guided missile, employing gyroscopic equipment.

It was after the war that he and his wife and children moved to a house on Atlantic Avenue on the edge of Garden City. Each day, when weather permitted, he commuted to his plant in Farmingdale in his small "Sperry Messenger" biplane, which he kept in a garage across the street. Residents in the area watched with wonder and delight as he took off from either Atlantic or Hilton Avenues, or landed the plane in the roughly mowed field (now Barnes Lane) nearby.

In 1923 he took his "Sperry Messenger" to Europe by boat to demonstrate its reliable and practical features. After a highly successful tour, bad weather over the English Channel in late December forced his light plane down, and the young flyer was drowned. The funeral services, later held in the Garden City Cathedral, were impressive and moving. Both during the service and at the cemetery, two formations of five Mitchel Field airplanes circled overhead, paying tribute to this remarkable young man and brilliant aviator.

14

THE THIRTIES AND FORTIES

Aviation activities in, around and over Garden City were destined to continue as a background to Village life, although in constantly changing forms. On June 23, 1931, the last great flight was made from Roosevelt Field, when Wiley Post and Harold Gatty left it to make a successful around-the-world flight in eight days. During the same year the Curtiss Engineering Company, planning to close its plant in Garden City, cancelled its lease at Roosevelt Field and transferred its experimental flying to a tract in Valley Stream.

In spite of these changes, Roosevelt Field, making the most of its excellent equipment, its flying schools, its passenger and freight express, continued to function throughout the 1930's as the most important commercial field in the east. It was only after LaGuardia Airport was completed in 1939 that the famous old field declined.

In the 1940's the spotlight swung to Mitchel Field, where, during World War II, thousands of army and transport planes were to leave its runways to fly over the Village of Garden City. Later still the Village was to hear the roar of commercial jets and superjets on their way to and from the Island's great commercial fields nearer New York City.

But back in the 1930's, the Incorporated Village of Garden City, unruffled by change, continued to grow and even to flourish. Financially, it had come through the depression of 1929 surprisingly well, in spite of its commitments in connection with the many permanent improvements it had made during the 1920's. That it was able to meet them without having to turn to the Reconstruction Finance Corporation or having to issue new bonds to meet outstanding bond maturities, was probably due to the steady commercial as well as residential growth of the Village and the farsighted planning and businesslike stewardship of the trustees.

Working out of a depression and providing services for a fast-growing population were to present constant problems, however. To keep residents informed and to report progress, the mayor and trustees of the Village published the first of Garden City's Annual Reports in 1931. Although it was largely a detailed financial report, it also included general information about Village administration, the Zoning and Planning Boards, legislation enacted during the year, and departmental activities. Except for 1933, there have been Annual Reports by successive mayors and trustees ever since, covering the same ground and happily providing a consecutive record of an always solvent, successful and outstanding community.

Garden City's population was to grow from 7,180 in 1930 to 14,364 in 1950, so it is not surprising that the Annual Reports reflect an acceleration and a continuing expansion of public services. In 1931 a second fire house was built on Stewart Avenue and Tanners Pond Road, new fire equipment purchased, five new police patrol cars ordered, and a storm sewer installed on Cherry Valley Avenue. In 1933 water trunk extensions were made, another new well built, a million-gallon water tower erected, and a new garbage incinerator constructed. This was to be the pattern to the present time.

It was during the 1930's that Village planning turned to the problem of parking. As early as 1931 licenses for parking at the five small station parking lots had been authorized, and by 1934 plans were under way not only to enlarge and improve these areas, but to provide adequate, free and well-landscaped interior parking zones behind all public and business areas. Opposition to what seemed an extravagant and unique step for such a small village was inevitable, but after several public meetings an agreement was reached that 8½ acres should be developed in the business, apartment and post office districts. The celebration of "Municipal Parking Week" in 1938, when these new fields were finally opened, put Garden City in the news not only in Nassau County but in Westchester and New Jersey suburbs as well. People came from far and near to drive into these well paved and carefully landscaped areas, to park their cars in safe rows, to shop, and to pick up their "Visitor's Contest" cards from local merchants in hopes of winning the Chamber of Commerce-sponsored prize of a 1938 Chevrolet.

Best and Company had chosen Garden City as the location for its first suburban branch in 1930, and now, with the promise of interior parking, built its own store on the corner of Franklin and Stewart Avenues. Other store units were soon in the planning and building stage; and in 1937 Loeser's large branch store, now owned by Abraham and Straus, started the northward trend up Franklin Avenue.

Along with business buildings, new apartment houses were going up too. The largest, Hilton Hall, a four-story 104-unit apartment complex to the east of the Hotel, was built in 1931, replacing two large "Apostle" houses which had been landmarks on that site since Mr. Stewart's time. That same year a subsidiary of the Doubleday Company petitioned for a zoning variance so that apartments could be built on Second Street, and in 1938 a large new apartment began to go up on Stewart Avenue, east of Franklin Avenue.

New houses were being built too all over the Village, especially in the Eastern Section, where the Mott Brothers were busily putting up the four hundred houses which probably led far-sighted Mayor Koons to predict that the Village was decidedly "in the path of a tidal wave of population."

This new housing coincided most conveniently with the completion in 1937 of Stewart School on Clinton Road. In the Estates Section, the School Board met the challenge by building another addition to Stratford School, and in Central Garden City, by overhauling and remodeling the Cathedral and Cherry Valley Schools to absorb the newly-accredited Junior and Senior High School classes.

Churches were equally forward-looking. In 1937 the Community Church bought and remodeled a large house on Stewart Avenue for temporary use until its Colonial church could be built nearby. The following year Bishop Stires's dream of a Cathedral House, providing an auditorium, diocesan headquarters and Sunday School classrooms came true. And in 1939 St. Joseph's Parochial School was completed on Fourth Street.

Garden City was not alone in feeling the effects of the encroaching "Tidal Wave." The County, finding its quarters in the Old County Court House too limited, broke ground in 1938 for its new P.W.A.-sponsored County Seat on Old Country Road and Washington Avenue. Originally designed as a seven-story structure, its plans now included a group of three 2½-story buildings to be located on the northern twenty-five acres of the Mineola Fair Grounds. This change had been forced on the County by Garden City's restrictive Zoning Ordinance, which, according to *The Nassau Daily Review Star*, "frequently appeared to be unduly harsh in its rulings."

This defeat of the County at the hands of Garden City was only one of the many zoning problems which the Village had to work out during the thirties and late forties. Outstanding were the weeks of study and conflict over the municipal parking project and the variances for apartment houses, the decisions concerning Fairchild's Funeral Home, the Curtiss Wright building and the Seventh Street Diner, and the rejection of the petition by the L.E.K. Oil Company to construct twelve 75,000-gallon gasoline and oil storage tanks on Commercial Avenue.

In 1937 the Village refused permission for a Franklin Avenue motion picture house between Fifth and Sixth Streets, and completed the zoning of all undeveloped areas in Garden City before the new County charter, giving the County jurisdiction over unclassified areas in incorporated villages, went into effect. A year later, Garden City successfully prevented the building of a seven-unit garden apartment south of the Cherry Valley Club on Cambridge Avenue, and, with the help of Club members, prevented the Garden City Country Club from becoming a 600-home housing development.

For six years during the thirties, the Village struggled, but less successfully, with another problem. This concerned the night-time dog racing which the Agricultural Society had introduced in 1932 at the Fair Grounds to defray its expenses. Immediately opposed by Garden City as a public nuisance, as unsportsmanlike and even as possibly illegal, the races, based on the 'option' or pari-mutuel system, nevertheless prospered on the tax-exempt track. Cheap beer halls and dance pavilions prospered too, attracting even greater crowds and causing one Long Island newspaper to beg its readers to fight the track and not let the area "go to the dogs."

Definite action was taken by the Village in 1936, when it sent its counselor to Albany, along with delegates from other affected communities in the State, to protest Assemblyman Leonard W. Hall's bill which had passed both houses and which favored dog racing in its existing form. Although the bill was vetoed by the Governor that year, a second one, hardly more favorable, passed the next. But by this time local pressure as well as County plans for the northern section of the Fair Grounds happily put an end to dog racing in Garden City.

Ironically enough, night-time racing flared up again two years later, but this time a mile to the east of the Village and under the more reliable auspices of the Old Country Trotting Association. Frustrated in its attempt to take over the dog racing track, the Association bought the extreme eastern portion of Roosevelt Airfield, which was no longer being used, laid out a track, and in 1940 celebrated its opening with a thirty-day meet. This was the first Roosevelt Raceway, later to be developed in its present form.

Another long struggle during the thirties was Garden City's attempt to find some alternative solution to the New York State Public Service Commission's plan to eliminate grade crossings by raising the railroad tracks throughout the Village. Faced with the possibility of an east-west Chinese Wall which would effectively bisect it, Garden City joined other neighboring villages equally threatened and hired an engineering expert to dream up some feasible solution. The subsequent Turner Report, fruit of two years' work, presented an almost equally drastic plan. Its chief features were the complete elimination of the railroad through Garden City from Floral Park to Clinton Road, the substitution of north-south bus services to new stations on the main line, a Central Garden City Station on the Hempstead-Mineola branch at Hempstead Crossing, and the building of a diagonal spur from the main line east of Mineola, through the northeast section of the Village, to join what was left of Mr. Stewart's railroad at Clinton Road on its way out to Bethpage Junction.

Luckily the financial aspects of the Commission's large-scale project, as well as concerted local opposition, provided some delay. But pressure was applied again both in 1935 and 1937, both times on a less ambitious scale. The end result in Garden City was the grade crossing elimination at Meadow Street, which was finally completed in 1943.

Probably the worst threat to Garden City came in 1948, when the State Department of Public Works revealed its plan for a six-lane raised expressway, another Chinese Wall, which was to run from Valley Stream diagonally northward through the Estates Section of Garden City, meet a spur from Douglaston, run parallel to Old Country Road, and then diagonally cross through Garden City's northeastern section on its way to Farmingdale and Riverhead. Not only would the proposed highway divide the Village into three areas and cause endless local transportation difficulties, but it would lower real estate values and eliminate sixty acres of private property by condemnation proceedings.

Protests were immediately filed by the Village Board of Garden City and by those in authority in other threatened communities, and every effort was made to have the proposed highway relocated. In this case local protests, condemnation expenses and other considerations prevailed, and the Long Island Expressway was later constructed as a direct highway through Queens and north-central Nassau, fortunately bypassing Garden City entirely.

Internal and external pressures and problems were to continue from this time on as parts of Village life, along with the air activity overhead. But these two decades of experience in such matters were to stand Garden City in good stead. During those twenty years mayors, trustees, Planning Boards, Boards of Zoning Appeals, Property Owners' Associations, the Chamber of Commerce, Rotary Club, Real Estate Boards, citizens' committees and individual residents, had all been involved in creating, over the years and for the future, a broad non-partisan pattern of considered action and concerted defense against unwanted change.

All this civic activity, however, still left a great deal of time for normal Village pursuits and pleasures; and as new residents came to live in Garden City, they were also soon involved in school, church and club affairs. Golf was undoubtedly one of the great attractions of the Village. As Frank Crowninshield wrote in 1936, when the 40th National Amateur Championship was being played on the Garden City Golf Club course, "the district around Garden City has become the most active golfing center in the United States. Within a radius of five miles from the spire of the Cathedral there are today more and better golf courses than in any district of the same area in America."

Other sports were equally available, from tennis, bowling and bad-minton at the Casino, to flying lessons at Roosevelt Field and ice skating on Hubbell's pond. And in 1937 Garden City even achieved a beach club at Atlantic Beach, with cabañas, bath-houses and a terraced blue and white club house overlooking the ocean.

By this time the "family car" had become an accepted adjunct to suburban life, making it easy and pleasant to run down to the new beach club, attend the polo matches at Meadow Brook, drop in at the Fair Grounds, drive to the Princeton-Yale game, and to enjoy the new State parkways which were being built on the Island. Mr. Vander-bilt's Motor Parkway was also still available during most of the thirties, but on Easter Day, 1938, it finally succumbed to competi-tion, post-depression hard times and to the demands of larger, faster and more numerous cars. From that time on its toll gates were closed and its roadbed deeded to the counties through which it ran. In Garden City, the attractive toll house was fortunately sold to the gate keeper, making for some continuity; but the manager's office was converted into a residence, and the steel and concrete bridge over Clinton Road dismantled. Mr. Vanderbilt's name was not for-gotten, however. In the late 1930's his nephew, George Vanderbilt, organized a new Cup Race, donated a new trophy, and built a new track at the east end of Roosevelt Airfield. And once more Garden City residents turned out to watch the "Vanderbilt Cup Races" and to compare the European Alfa Romeos, Maseratis, and Mercedes Benzes with the competing American cars.

Events on Long Island have always attracted great crowds. In 1939, Garden City families were driving to the New York World's Fair in Flushing Meadows, where, along with thousands of other enthusiastic families, they could gaze at the Trylon and Perisphere, eat strange foods in foreign restaurants, gape at the British Crown Jewels, enjoy the fireworks, and exclaim over "World of Tomorrow" displays.

But before the Fair was over, World War II had begun in Europe, and by 1941 had involved the United States. The story of Garden City during those four tragic years is, by and large, the story of every other village, suburb and small town in the country—a story of complete civilian mobilization for the war effort. If not in the armed services, American men and women worked on Draft Boards, Rationing Boards or Civil Emergency Committees; headed up Red Cross activities and Bond Drives; drove ambulances, learned 'pressure points,' or worked in hospitals. Others organized car-pools, collected scrap iron and paper, knitted, sewed, or became air raid wardens. Quite a few took their turns on lonely towers or steeples as airplane spotters.

As in World War I, Garden City citizens had the added excitement and emotional impact of living next to a great Army base—this time Mitchel Field. Once more trains from New York were full of young men in uniform, and the "dinkey" shuttle from Country Life Press station was packed to the doors. Once more the sad lonely sound of "taps" could be heard at night in the Eastern Section of the Village. But this time, instead of the flickering light of camp fires to the east, there were the probing sweeps of airplane beacons, and instead of the few fragile planes of the last war, the skies over Garden City were full of the powerful fighters, bombers and transport planes of World War II.

In May 1945 Germany surrendered, and three months later, Japan. The Allies had won the war, but at a staggering cost of life. Garden City's memorial tablet alone lists 44 war dead.

Post-war years in the Village were concerned chiefly with adjusting to more normal circumstances, and to preparing for the boom in business, industry and population which seemed inevitable for central Long Island. In fact, the boom had already started during the war, when the rapid development of the airplane industry had started a mass migration from city to suburb. Literally thousands of men and women had moved out to work at the Grumman, Sperry, Republic, Liberty and Fairchild plants. Now most of them were staying; and the returning veterans, eager for drastic change and a better life, were joining them in their search for housing and employment.

Garden City's location, in the center of what was to become the fastest-growing county in the United States, called for prompt planning and action. As usual, the Board of Trustees had not been idle, and a month after the Japanese surrender in 1945, it was able to report on the "Comprehensive Study" of the Village which it had authorized. Zoning ordinances had been reviewed and strengthened, and plans for a controlled housing and business expansion had been suggested.

The trustees also took definite action for immediate improvements in Garden City. By 1948, plans were being made for connections with the County Sewer System; a site for a larger Village Hall and Fire House had been acquired on Stewart Avenue, and a second major parking-field project had been launched.

The last two years of the 1940's were busy and prosperous ones in the Village generally. Houses began to sprout on empty lots, Franklin Simon built on Ninth Street, Abraham & Straus added a big wing, and Franklin Avenue real estate soared in value. To the west, scaffolding sheathed the Cathedral spire for a much-needed repair job, and the Hotel went through another bout of redecorating and expansion, this time at the hands of the Knott Hotel Corporation, which leased and later bought it from the Garden City Company. In the Eastern Section, Custer Park on Commercial Avenue was graded and seeded, and the old Curtiss Wright plant made ready for the Oxford Filing Supply Company. The boom had started, and Garden City, which had celebrated its successful past at its Diamond Jubilee in 1944, now confidently faced the future.

15

THE FIFTIES

"No community can live alone. Each is a part of the County, which in turn is part of the huge metropolitan complex with its great forces of population, economic activity and community development." This excerpt from the 1959 Annual Report sums up Garden City's situation during the ten challenging years of the fifties, when Nassau County's spectacular growth and development were to affect even the most carefully planned and safeguarded village.

During those years, Nassau County's population doubled and all its physical and governmental aspects changed. Terms such as "crash growth," "population explosion," "decentralization of industry," "county control," "regional shopping centers," "housing and school shortages," and "super highways and pretzel approaches," came into common usage. And as old landmarks and empty fields vanished, county and village residents began to talk and read about Levittown, research laboratories, Arma and Airborne, branch banks, computers, electronics, plastics, concrete block construction, and traffic hazards.

Physically Garden City was largely protected on three sides by established communities, but it had already found itself vulnerable on its eastern boundaries, where airfields, Army installations and race tracks had been established on the unincorporated areas of the great empty Plains. Now, in the fifties, industry and business were to establish themselves as well, and almost overnight factories, laboratories, gas stations and office buildings began to go up along the roads and highways to the east and north of the Village.

Before long it became generally known that Webb & Knapp, Inc., had bought the 360 acres which had formerly comprised Roosevelt Field and Old Westbury Golf Course, and under the name of Roosevelt Field, Inc., proposed to develop the eastern 180 acres as a planned industrial center, and the western 180 as one of the largest and most complete regional shopping centers in the East.

This brought industry and business to Garden City's very doorstep and, in fact, within its doors, since fifty-five of the western acres of the famous old airfield, bordering on Clinton Road, were within the limits of the Village. Neglected and overgrown, this triangular fringe area, occupied only by a few tumble-down hangars but zoned for residences, almost immediately became the bone of contention between the Village and the new Corporation, which in 1954 petitioned to have it rezoned for its commercial purposes.

The first reaction in the Village, especially in the Eastern Section, was instinctively against rezoning, especially as the Corporation's plan included an exit-entrance on Clinton Road. The Chamber of Commerce, feeling that business interests in Garden City would suffer, was equally opposed. But as all the facts and alternatives became known, a more considered reaction began to emerge. The Roosevelt Shopping Center would be built in any case; traffic would inevitably increase, and the successful and safe development of the small isolated tract as a residential area would be impossible.

The problem obviously called for time and dispassionate study. During the next nine months planning experts and lawyers were consulted, existing Village organizations and commissions were called on to examine the situation, and public hearings were held. By the end of the year it was generally agreed that compromise was the only solution; and in February 1955 the Village Board, in accordance with the wishes of all four Property Owners' Associations, unanimously approved the greatly modified application of the Roosevelt Field Corporation for rezoning the area under special restrictions. These hard-fought and vital restrictions provided that there were to be no exits or entrances on Clinton Road; that a 70-foot landscaped buffer strip along its eastern border was to be deeded to the Village; that the area was to be limited to three-story professional or business buildings with minimum land coverage and 232-foot set-backs; that brightly-lit signs were to be outlawed; and that the unsightly hangars were to be removed.

Within a few years the huge shopping center had become a reality and the fifty-five acres an integral, though not fully developed, part of the carefully planned and landscaped project. Garden City, although still sensitive to the situation, was becoming increasingly aware as time went on that there had been no satisfactory alternative and that the Village's balanced residential-economic planning for the future had not been destroyed by the rezoning. Some further comfort could be found in the fact that Meadow Brook Parkway, recently completed, bisected the Corporation's vast development, and was effectively draining off a great deal of the dreaded north-south traffic.

Within Garden City itself, the 1950's brought almost as many changes as in the County. During those ten years the Village, too, all but doubled its population, from 14,364 in 1950 to 23,837 in 1960; 2,567 new residences and 261 apartment units were built; public services were rapidly stepped up to meet the demand; Fire and Police Departments were enlarged, and four new schools were built.

Franklin Avenue, meanwhile, made great strides in fulfilling its promise of becoming an outstanding 'quality' shopping and business street, as the Medical Center, the Garden City Company-Stouffer Building, the Suburbia Federal Savings Bank, Lord & Taylor, the new Best and Peck & Peck stores, and other smaller business buildings, went up on either side. A crowning touch was added in 1960 when Saks Fifth Avenue leased the site next to Lord & Taylor's for a branch store, and publicized the street as "The Fifth Avenue of Long Island." Still farther north, large new County buildings, this time permitted to soar beyond the three-story limit, began to change the sky line along Old Country Road.

Vacant land on Seventh Street disappeared as well. As soon as the old Village Hall and Fire House had been demolished, a new A & P quickly filled the void, only to be challenged on the east by a large Gristede store and the promise of a Bohack's across the street. Other smaller business buildings went up to the west, and the bank building was enlarged and had a complete face-lifting.

Eighth Street, or rather Stewart Avenue West, now became the focal point of the community as the new Village Hall, a far cry from the old converted stable, neared completion in 1953. Large, dignified and handsome, the new building dramatized, as nothing else could have done, the growth and maturity of the Village.

Away from the center of Garden City, in its outlying sections, changes also took place with surprising rapidity. Empty parcels of land gave way not only to houses but to churches and schools. St. Anne's Parochial School and Convent were completed in the 50's, the Community Church was dedicated in 1951, the Garden City Nursery School was built in 1957, and a large wing of St. Joseph's School was begun in 1960. The Jewish Center was established in 1953, a new Lutheran Church was built on Stewart Avenue, and the School of Theology of the Episcopal Diocese of Long Island, under the administration of Bishop James P. DeWolfe, who had succeeded Bishop Stires in 1942, joined the other buildings on the Cathedral grounds. Adelphi, which had grown from a small women's college to a large coeducational one since it had moved to Garden City, added new dormitories and science buildings to its campus in 1956, and broke ground in 1960 for its exciting "Living Library." On the southern acres of the campus, the Waldorf School, offering classes from nursery through high school, also expanded rapidly.

Public school construction reached a peak during this period of tremendous Village growth. In fact the completion of the three K3 neighborhood schools in 1959 put the finishing touches to Garden City's outstanding school facilities. Looking back, there can be no doubt that the Village had started late in this field. Depending on the two excellent Cathedral Church Schools and on Hempstead's High School, Garden City had drifted along with one inadequate school house until 1923, when citizen demand and Hempstead's crowded condition had forced the School Board to act. But once started the Village had fallen into its usual pattern of doing a job well. By 1940 it had provided not only a large central school besides the old Cathedral Avenue school, but also two fine elementary schools, and had already earned, through its fine teaching and administrative staffs, a reputation for high standards and sound college preparation all over the eastern seaboard.

In 1953 the Village had at last achieved a new high school—a rambling, red-brick building on Merillon Avenue, which included excellent class-room and laboratory facilities, a library, cafeteria, gymnasium and an all-purpose auditorium big enough for symphony concert use. A year later the Junior High School had been doubled in size to satisfy the needs of that particular student age group.

New buildings are not enough to account for the early and continued success of Garden City's public school system. Primarily responsibile are its unusually fine teachers and its homogeneous and ambitious student body. Another helpful feature has been the fact that the Village, since its incorporation, has been all but coterminus with the School District. This has undoubtedly simplified the job of building up a smooth-running system over the years, and of creating a congenial and single-minded attitude for successive School Boards. The method of choosing members of these successive Boards from the four sections of the Village has been equally helpful, and has made for the same non-partisan planning and administration that has worked out so well in Village government. As usual, the unsung heroes are the taxpayers who have cooperated throughout the years in this success. Not one school budget has been turned down in Garden City.

The increased need for schools in Garden City and in other villages throughout the County, was only one result of the population explosion of the 1950's. Another was the need for added recreational facilities. The County had luckily made a good start during the last decade by cooperating with the State in providing large public recreational playgrounds such as the Bethpage and Hempstead Lake Parks, and Jones Beach. During the 50's it also continued the development of Salisbury Park as its largest County playground, an area which had once been part of the Stewart purchase and which had more recently, from 1916 to 1928, been owned and operated by the Lannin Realty Company as a public subscription golf course.

Nassau villages were slower to face the situation; by 1960 fewer than a dozen had provided recreational programs of their own. To its credit, Garden City was one of the first, having formed its Recreation Commission, headed by a full-time supervisor, in 1956. That same

The newly-built Cathedral on its high bare site, with St. Paul's School in the background, 1885.

The Cathedral as it is today.

year the Village added new neighborhood playgrounds, extended its park areas, and built its highly successful modern swimming pool on south Cherry Valley Avenue. Open only to Garden City residents, the pool has been run since that time as a self-supporting enterprise under the efficient and imaginative control of the Commission. Consisting actually of three pools, the swimming pool has become the most popular place in the Village during the summer months, catering as it does to the infant population with its wading pool, to children and teenagers with its Olympic-sized pool, and to adults with its "middle-sized" one. Its popularity extends into evening hours as well, when, on special nights, the Commission arranges for swimming meets, water polo, square dancing or movies.

In spite of the success of the pool, a similar but more expensive project—that of providing for an all-year-round recreational Community Center—was defeated in a "Town Meeting" vote in 1959. To compensate, all weekend recreational programs have been stepped up, and the schools and churches have cooperated as well.

Garden City's private recreational clubs took action in the late 1950's, too. Not only was the Casino enlarged, but both the Cherry Valley and Garden City Golf Clubs terminated their leases with the Garden City Company and bought their respective properties. Since the Garden City Country Club also owns its land, these three clubs now provide ample recreational opportunities for adults, and also provide three large and beautiful park-like areas within the Village, which are at least temporarily safe from redevelopment as homes.

A great addition to Garden City's recreational and cultural life came in 1952, when the Village achieved a library of its own. After years of unsuccessful effort on the part of individuals, committees and organizations, a group of resourceful and practical women took a preparatory course in library procedures and then set up a small experimental library in an unused cottage on Seventh Street, which the Village had loaned them for the purpose. Operated and supported by volunteer effort for three years, it proved so indispensable that, by a referendum vote in 1955, it became a tax-supported public library under Village control.

Armed with a budget, a provisional charter from the State, and a full-time trained librarian, the little library soon became even more popular and crowded as additional books, students and eager borrowers filled the small rooms. A larger building was obviously a necessity, and the following year the Village purchased the centrally-located Garden City Company office and its site in the park, as the Library's permanent home. Funds were provided for its renovation and for the addition of a large wing, which was later appropriately named the Hubbell Wing in honor of Mr. and Mrs. George L. Hubbell. The park surrounding the building was also deeded to the Village at this time through the generosity of the Garden City Company, and has subsequently been called Memorial Park in honor of Garden City's enlisted men and women of World War II.

Due to citizen interest, the Village also became involved in two successful international projects in the early 1950's. One occurred when Garden City joined with Coburg, Germany, and Aix-en-Provence, France, in an international good-will program called "Operation-Town-Affiliation," for the exchange of ideas, correspondence, visitors, and possibly students. The second project involved cooperation with an organization called "The Experiment in International Living," which concerned itself chiefly with the actual exchange of students.

Two Garden City students, in fact, made summer trips to Europe that first year under the joint auspices of these organizations—a beginning which later developed into a growing and continuing exchange on a wider scale, enabling small groups of foreign students to live and study with American students in the Village, and groups of Garden City students to experience home and village life in Europe.

Both programs are still in operation. The second, now called the Garden City International Student Exchange, has involved hundreds of Village families over the years. Originally made possible by private subscription, it is now largely supported by the Community Fund, with help from the Rotary Club, and has proved to be one of the most stimulating and rewarding projects undertaken by the Village.

The Community Fund itself was also organized during the 50's. Run by a committee representing the four sections of the Village, it has proved to be still another example of successful citizen cooperation, involving in this case over a thousand volunteers for each drive. Due to its efficient management, the Fund effectively and almost painlessly collects the required funds for its carefully selected causes.

Garden City was now almost a hundred years old, and had the

stamp of a successful and well-adjusted community. It had fulfilled the plans of its founder, Alexander Stewart, who in 1869 wrote to the people of Hempstead Township that he would develop the land for settlers and would erect fine buildings and residences "so that a barren waste may be speedily covered by a population desirable in every respect as neighbors, taxpayers, and citizens." The settlement was now a beautiful village, and its population, though larger than he might have imagined, was worthy of his vision.

Garden City, in its well-loved Cathedral and Church Schools, had also fulfilled Mrs. Stewart's plans for a memorial to her husband. In other ways the Village reflected the worldly yet practical planning of the heirs who had controlled and developed it for twenty-six years with the help of Mr. Hubbell. Best of all, the Village justified the continued participation of its citizens, who without remuneration had governed it as an incorporated community since 1919.

Perhaps the 1950s represented a high point in Garden City's history. Pressures from without and within had mounted, due to the rapid growth of the country and village itself. Competition from new shopping centers and discount houses posed problems, traffic was increasing alarmingly, and the inflated economy was straining budgets. Even the cherished Garden City Hotel was suffering from the competition of nearby motels and restaurants.

16

THE SIXTIES

Garden City's ability to meet change was to be tried and tested during the sixties when, in 1962, rumors that the Garden City Hotel might be in trouble became a reality. That year the Knott Hotel Corporation, which had bought the Hotel and its twenty-one-acre park in 1948 from The Garden City Company for $800,000, had spent $1,600,000 in improvements, and had run it as a quality hotel for over a decade, admitted that it could no longer make ends meet and was in fact losing over $100,000 a year.

Rather than abandoning the venture entirely, the Corporation asked the Village Board of Trustees for a change in zoning to permit the building of two three-story apartments on either side of the Hotel, which, they promised, would also be improved. As garden apartments, set well back from the street and embedded in the park, they were to contain sixty-two units each, would be provided with underground parking and with tunnels leading to the Hotel.

Although in retrospect the plans sound ideal, Garden City was not ready for such drastic departure. The very word "apartments" in connection with the famous Hotel and its park was unthinkable. Tradition, reputation, and local pride had to be considered as well as concern for the Village as a whole. Questions too came to mind. Would this precedent encourage further unwanted development? Would Garden City go the way of Forest Hills, Hempstead, and less fortunate communities? Before long County and even New York newspapers took up the cry of dismay. One particular article in *Newsday,* titled "Where History Was a Guest," seemed to speak for everyone in expressing regret for a "past and now-lost splendor."

In a calmer and more dispassionate manner the Board of Trustees, the Property Owners Associations, and the Board of Zoning Appeals deliberated, reviewed citizen opinion, consulted multi-housing experts, but eventually turned down the application as unacceptable.

The Hotel was now for sale at $2,100,000 and many hoped that the Village would consider buying it even if it meant a long-range tax burden. But in 1965 a serious offer was made by the respectable De Matteis Development Corporation of Elmont to buy the property and, if a zoning variance could be obtained, raze the Hotel and build a nine-story E-shaped hotel-apartment complex on the site. It was to contain 150 hotel rooms, a banquet hall and 450 apartment units — the estimated cost to be $17,000,000.

Citizen outcry against this plan was even greater and less restrained than before. All the old arguments surfaced and new ones were added. It was felt that such a large complex would result in a "mass invasion" of new citizens in the center of the Village, that so many apartments would upset the balance of land use, that traffic would double, and that a nine-story skyscraper would be aesthetically intolerable.

Trustees and all responsible Village organizations once more had to face the issues. The result was the same and, in October 1965, copies of *Village Facts* were sent to all homeowners outlining the negative decision — namely, a denial of the application for rezoning since "the proposal would be detrimental to the surrounding area of the Village as a whole." That same year the property was sold to a construction firm headed by Michael Forte for $1,800,000. The new owner promised to repair the Hotel and return it to its former elegance and prestige.

Hopes ran high when the plans were revealed. A new corporation called The Garden City Hotel Corporation had been formed with Mr. Forte as Chairman of the Board, and with Delmonico's Mr. John L. Webber, an internationally famous hotel manager, as president and director. Loans from the Chemical Bank of New York had been arranged, and an architect had been engaged. Extensive renovations and modernizations were to make it once again a ranking hotel of distinction for the social and business communities of Nassau County.

During the first year various cosmetic improvements were made. The lobby and halls were repainted and refurnished and, after suitable publicity, the Regency Room was completely redecorated by former Duke Arturo Pini di San Miniato, an internationally known designer. It emerged a handsome room, suitable not only for large luncheons, but inviting for small formal balls with its sky blue ceiling, adorned with fleecy white clouds, and its row of gilt chairs flanking the tall satin-draped windows.

Nearby in the popular Hunt Room a large circular bar was installed; and soon cocktail and luncheon napkins, menus, letter paper and china, all elegantly embossed with the Stewart Crest, were available for use. In the dining areas crisp white and carefully chosen pastel linens, delivered by Rolls-Royce, graced the tables in the new Colonial Room as well as on the outdoor terrace in summer.

During the relatively short time that Mr. Webber was in charge, improvements were varied and impressive. His untimely death, however, prevented major long-range plans and basic changes from being carried out. The high hopes of a completely revitalized hotel declined from then on as the usual problems of running a large ninety-year-old hotel multiplied.

During this period there were naturally other events important to the Village. One was the colorful ceremony which took place just east of the Hotel to celebrate the three-hundredth anniversary of the first organized horse racing in America — at Newmarket Course on the Hempstead Plains.

Sponsored and arranged by the New York Racing Association, the program included a fanfare, a uniformed fife and drum corps, a group of Adelphi students in Colonial garb, speeches, proclamations, and the unveiling of a handsome bronze plaque, which the Association presented to the Mayor on behalf of the Village of Garden City. Backed by landscaped planting, it stands on the south-west corner of the Village Hall park at Stewart and Hilton Avenues and reads:

1665–1965

THE FIRST FORMAL RACE MEET IN THE UNITED STATES TOOK PLACE NEAR HERE ON "HAMPSTED PLAINES" UNDER THE SPONSORSHIP OF COLONIAL GOVERNOR NICOLLS IN 1665

Colonial Governor Richard Nicolls at the Hempstead Plains race course, 1665. (The Bettmann Archive)

Along with the telegrams from important County and State well-wishers was a message from Queen Elizabeth. "I am glad," she graciously wrote, "to think that horse racing, which started under the orders of a British Governor of New York, has continued to flourish in the United States, forging a further link between those in both countries who are interested in thoroughbred breeding and in the sport of racing. I send my greetings to all who will be joining in celebrating this anniversary." Such a prestigious communication called for the release of the three hundred red, white, and blue balloons which ended the festivities.

In spite of rising costs, construction in the Village continued, producing the Long Island Trust Company's new Administration Building on Franklin Avenue, and three office buildings on East Seventh Street which were to provide space for even more insurance companies. Across the Avenue the modern Texaco station replaced the old brick garage — a veritable landmark — which from 1908 on had catered to cars and drivers dating back to Vanderbilt Cup Race and Motor Parkway days.

The most impressive addition to the Village was the completion in

1966 of the New York State Supreme Court Building erected by Nassau County at the cost of $11,000,000 as part of the complex of County buildings. Designed by the firm of Chapman, Evans and Delahanty, the four-story granite and marble building contains a central jury room and courtrooms and chambers for twenty-seven judges. It covers a gross 194,000 square feet — a far cry from the small Victorian cupola-crowned Exhibition Hall of the Queens County Agricultural Society, which had stood on the same site when Garden City was built.

At about the same time a new Unitarian Church in the Estate Section replaced the old Gage Tarbell home, which Glenn Curtiss had once owned. Both St. Paul's and St. Mary's added wings to their Schools, and Adelphi University's Student Union was under construction.

Village improvements included the widening of Nassau Boulevard, the development of two new recreation areas, and the building of a larger municipal garage. Worries continued concerning the future of Mitchel Field, the extension of Oak Street, and the grim possibility — later rejected — of a "County Boulevard" using the old railroad right-of-way from Mineola to West Hempstead.

Of far greater concern to Garden City was the undeclared and divisive Vietnam War, which made the sixties a decade of despair, anger, and frustration for all America. Once more the youth of the Village were called on to fight in a foreign land. The plaques in Memorial Park bear witness to their continued response.

As a much-needed antidote, 1969 heralded the Hundredth Anniversary of the Founding of Garden City. Always known for careful planning, the Village outdid even itself in celebrating this year-long event under the guidance of a large enthusiastic committee representing all Village and business organizations, clubs, churches, and schools.

A Stewart Centennial Ball seemed to be the obvious way to begin the festivities. On the night of February 22 over a thousand residents came to the still-elegant Garden City Hotel to dine and dance in the three professionally-decorated ballrooms, to watch a "Victorian" Fashion Show, to welcome the parade of waiters carrying individual birthday cakes for each table, to drink to Garden City's past and future, and to welcome special guests.

One of these was C. Walter Randall, who had hammered out the

"Gentlemen's Agreement" so successfully in 1919. Others were members of the Hubbell clan, Devereux Emmet, Mrs. William Langmore, and other relatives of the Stewart-Clinch family. Toasts, speeches, prayers, and historical anecdotes were inevitably part of the evening's entertainment — as was the playing of "Good Night, Ladies" at the end of one of Garden City's most delightful community events.

The proceeds of the Ball had been earmarked for a Memorial to Alexander Stewart, and although there was some disagreement as to the form it should take, the final decision was for commissioning a bronze bust of the Founder to whom the Village owed its existence. Those favoring a gift toward a new public library were naturally disappointed — a small elite band of Senior High School students especially, who expressed their feelings by parading their placards reading "Get Ahead — Not a Head," "Busts Are for Pigeons," "Ever Done a Term Paper with a Statue?"

When actual plans for the Memorial were revealed, however, it was a comfort to know that a distinguished sculptor, Granville W. Carter, N.A., who had just completed the prizewinning *West Texas Pioneer Family* and had several busts in the Hall of Fame to his credit, had been commissioned.

The bust was to be of bronze, half life size, and would depict Mr. Stewart in his middle years, as the Rossiter portrait in the public library represented him. The pedestal was to be an eight-foot section of one of the facade-supporting columns of the razed Pennsylvania Station, which, like the Hotel, had been designed by McKim, Mead and White. A small circular park area, in what is now Hubbell Plaza, was appropriately chosen as the site for the Memorial.

Mr. Stewart was also honored pictorially when the Mineola–Garden City Rotary Club had Commemorative Medals struck — his profile on the obverse side and the Village Seal on the other. The Seal also appeared on the newly-designed official Flag of Garden City which the Jaycees sponsored and later sold in miniature with the help of Junior High School students. This school also contributed a slide history of the Village, based on photographs from the Garden City Archives, and published a delightfully illustrated *Garden City: A History for Children,* written by Arlene Olson.

Other publications consisted of a folder, "1869-1969," by the Chamber of Commerce, an updated booklet, "Know Garden City,"

Granville W. Carter at work on the bust of Alexander Turney Stewart in 1969.

by the League of Women Voters, and the 1969 "Village Annual Report," containing a nostalgic photo-history of the Village with text by John Orban. Written especially for the Centennial was Vincent F. Seyfried's *The Founding of Garden City,* which, like his L.I.R.R. books, has become an invaluable source.

The highlight of the year's celebration proved to be Centennial Week spanning October 12th through the 18th. It started with a pancake breakfast at Adelphi, followed by an Ecumenical Church Service at the Cathedral of the Incarnation — itself a memorial to Mr. Stewart. Good weather favored an outdoor Sidewalk Art Show as well as a Fashion Show and Luncheon at the Hotel; and competition raged during the week for prizes for the best "historical" store window displays on Seventh Street and Franklin Avenue.

One of the gayest events was the Hundredth Anniversary Party, sponsored by the four Property Owners Associations for the benefit of the Public Library Fund. Held in the Hotel, a banjo band, a barbershop quartet, balloons, straw hats, and the Walter Leege orchestra set the tone for the evening. Over $12,000 was raised, which was later added to by an equal gift from the Stewart Ball Committee.

The week ended on a beautiful October day with a "Homecoming" Parade followed by the dedication of the Stewart Memorial bust. A large crowd watched the huge crane set the circular foundation stone, lift the pedestal into position, and gingerly lower the head, which the sculptor had brought from his studio in a truck, into place. The serene face of the Founder of Garden City seems to look out at his handywork. He faces west so as to catch the best light, but also to face toward New York City, the pole star of all suburbs.

A few days later the Kiwanis Club buried a capsule, containing suitable documents and artifacts, at the base of the statue. And by the end of the year the Garden City Postal Cancellation of 1969 could no longer be used.

17

THE SEVENTIES

Although the United States had achieved the brilliant feat of putting a man on the moon only five months before, the seventies were to be difficult years, clouded by the continuing Vietnam War, the marches and riots, "Kent State," "Watergate," inflation, unemployment, racial tensions, and a resulting loss of confidence and hope.

Like all villages, towns, and cities, Garden City shared this general malaise and even had additional troubles of its own. One gratifying event, however, started off the decade when, in 1971, a referendum was voted on in favor of a new and adequate Public Library; a special Village election authorized a bond issue to cover the expense; and plans were actually being made for the new building.

The site was to be in the same Village-owned park just east of the existing facility, which when razed was to provide sufficient parking, and deep setbacks were planned to give the low, functional brick building the dignified surroundings it deserved. A groundbreaking ceremony in which two Junior High School students shared the honors with the Mayor soon followed; and in 1973 the entire Village joyfully celebrated the dedication of its new Library, which from the start had been an educational and cultural boon to the community. Credit must be given to the Garden City Exchange, the strong fund-raising arm of the Friends of the Garden City Public Library, for helping to make this project a reality.

During the same period, the largest suburban branch of New York's famous Bloomingdale's Department Store was being built on Franklin Avenue. Designed by Edward Durrell Stone, it is a handsome contemporary building of precast concrete stone, with a cantilevered garden balcony. A new feature for Garden City is the successful multi-level parking structure for twelve hundred cars, a convenience to shoppers and one which eliminates the need for another vast parking field.

The new Theodore Roosevelt Building along with two smaller office buildings soon filled in the space across the avenue, and on Seventh Street the need for apartments near the "family" shopping area was met by an attractive four-story condominium.

But satisfaction in these improvements could not offset the growing concern about the Hotel which, it was rumored, was in deep financial trouble and might even be closed. At midnight on July 15, 1971, this suddenly happened — an event as shocking to Garden City as the closing of the Cathedral doors would have been. As news spread through the Village, citizens flocked to the overcrowded Hunt Room to drown their sorrows and to sing "should auld acquaintance be forgot." Others came early the next morning to find the forlorn and worried group of elderly "permanent guests" all but homeless. Already chairs in the lobby and on the porches had been removed, most of the staff dismissed, and the kitchens and bar closed. Harassed relatives and friends were milling about, telephones were in constant demand, and eager reporters were everywhere.

At a press conference the next day, Mr. Forte, although he failed to explain the abruptness of the closing, presented his reasons. Reading slowly from a prepared statement, he said he had decided on closing the Hotel after Village police and fire marshals declared the upper floors unsafe for habitation. He went on to say that the structure was "physically and economically obsolete," that the layout, with its numerous entrances and stairwells, made security and crowd control almost impossible, and that his payroll and expenses were disproportionate to the gross income, resulting in losses he could no longer afford to absorb. He also added that the Hotel could no longer compete with modern hotels, motels, and restaurants.

As for the property, Forte would only say that it was not for sale, and that he might have a plan for its development later on. "I'm in love with this property, and this property will be developed in the right way," were his final words to a group of reporters.

During the next two weeks a skeleton staff struggled to find apartments or homes for the dispossessed guests, and to satisfy the $900,000 worth of banquet and catering contracts already accepted for the coming year. The large dinner in honor of Bishop Baldwin for that very week was taken over by Carl Hoppel, but relocating the many luncheons, charitable events, political dinners, and wedding receptions presented endless difficulties, compromises, and heartaches.

The rest of that painful summer was spent in selling off the entire contents of the Hotel. Crowds came from far and near to buy furniture, damask window draperies, crystal chandeliers, TV sets, kitchen equipment, dining room china, and even the lobby's imported Italian fireplace mantel. Competition was especially keen for the coveted black horse's head from the Hunt Room and for the nameplate on the door of the "Lindbergh Suite," which with its furniture was also in surprising demand. Among the milling crowds, residents of Garden City wandered sadly about, choosing nostalgic items which, as one of them said, were really "Memories for Sale." When it was finally over, the dismantled Hotel, a mere shell, stood forlorn and stripped in its acres of neglected lawns, weed-grown shrubbery, and age-old trees.

Since Mr. Forte's press release after the closing had failed to present alternative plans for the property, the Village, already briefed by the Mayor's Advisory Committee on the Hotel, now appointed a special five-man Redevelopment Board to explore possible options and to make recommendations. The basic one to emerge was that the neglected site be acquired by the Village either by purchase or condemnation, be rezoned for hotel and apartments, and be developed in a restricted and appropriate fashion with no more than a 10 percent land use.

In September, however, Forte presented his own plans. Encouraged by the success of his three huge Miami "Forte Towers" containing 1,600 apartments, he could only think in terms of "bigger is better." Accordingly, his proposal for Garden City was a complex, to be called "Forte Plaza," consisting of a 14-story, 700-room Convention hotel flanked by 12-story office buildings, two apartment towers to the rear, and underground parking for 3,250 cars. Estimated land coverage would be 26 percent, and the cost about $70,000,000.

Confrontation was now inevitable; and newspapers, architects, Property Owners Associations, a well-organized Preservation Committee, and other existing organizations eagerly clamored to participate and express their opinions. The first clash came when the Village barred Mr. Forte's plan, and he in turn strove to stop condemnation, to force rezoning for his plan, and to seek damages for carrying charges on the Hotel since its closing.

Although Mr. Forte was not successful in his efforts, some solution had to be attempted. Under severe pressure, when stakes are high, and unalterable circumstances exist, zoning can protect only so far. In this case, the site was privately owned by a developer who refused to sell; the owner was entitled to a fair return on his property and the Village a tax-productive return on its use; unbiased experts had pronounced the Hotel physically and economically obsolete; Landmark designation had been discouraged by the State; and a need for apartments existed. In addition, the possibility of a State or Federal takeover of the unused and neglected site could not be ignored.

In October 1972, more than a year after the closing of the Hotel, and after many confrontations, conferences, and recommendations from experts, the Village Board of Trustees under advisement of the Redevelopment Board, the Planning Commission, the Advisory Committee on Zoning, and the endorsement of the four Property Owners Associations unanimously passed a resolution implementing the rezoning of the Hotel site for a restricted hotel-apartment complex. It permitted a full-service hotel of 500 rooms, not more than 305 apartments, and a maximum height of 100 feet with a 250-foot setback.

Forte, who had already modified his plans somewhat, now set his architects to work in complying with the new zoning provisions, and in March 1973 a model of the complex was presented to the uneasy public. Its very size inevitably led to concern about traffic congestion, police and fire protection and environmental damage, and its tall buff-colored brick buildings seemed to cover far too much of the site and to challenge the conservative taste of the Village.

The strict building code and rigid specifications had been met, however, and in 1974 the plans were approved and a Demolition Permit to raze the Hotel was issued. It took months for the wrecker's ball to reduce the huge building to rubble, and months more to clear the site, cut down the trees, remove the top soil and glacial-outwash gravel, and to prepare the deep excavation. Although work on the foundations actually started that summer, it steadily diminished and finally ceased altogether.

The Manufacturers Hanover Trust Company foreclosed Mr. Forte's large mortgage in 1976. Instead of the advertised auction for its disposal, Myron Nelkin of the Fairhaven Management Company, holder of a small second mortgage, acquired it by "right of redemption," paid off all other liens on the property, and for a total of $5,200,000 became owner of the Garden City site.

A landmark's last days, 1973. (David Nernoff)

When Mr. Nelkin presented his own plans for the property, he asked for further zoning amendments to permit a smaller hotel of 240 rooms instead of 500, an increase in the number of condominiums from 305 to 396, a larger floor area to accommodate these changes, and setbacks to be adjusted in accordance with the height of the buildings. In September 1979 the Village Board of Trustees voted to approve these changes after receiving notification that the Nassau County Planning Commission made no objections. Almost immediately, heavy machinery came to clean up the littered excavation, and to bury or remove the useless cement foundation blocks and rusted steel beams so that future construction could begin.

Shocked by the destruction of the Hotel, a group of nine concerned women organized the Garden City Historical Society, dedicated to the cause of preserving as much of the remaining heritage of the Village as possible. Immediately popular, it soon received the status of a citizen-supported organization, obtained a charter, and a symbolic project to work for.

This was to rescue one of the oldest and most prestigious houses in the Village — a large, elegant "Apostle" house, built by Mr. Stewart in 1874. Used for years as an adjunct to St. Mary's School, it was no longer needed, had deteriorated from neglect, and had become a financial burden to the Episcopal Diocese to which it had been deeded "in perpetuity" by Mrs. Stewart. In 1975, by agreement with the Diocese, this landmark on Fifth Street was turned over to the Society, in lieu of rent, to improve, protect, and use. Within two years the house had been repaired and refurbished both inside and out, and now lends itself as a charming, homelike place for meetings, art exhibits, historical tours and lectures, as well as for summer picnics in its Victorian garden.

One important accomplishment of the Society was the tabulation of the many historic buildings in Central Garden City, and their subsequent listing in 1978 on the National Register of Historic Places as "The A. T. Stewart Era Buildings." This honor places no restrictions on the forty odd houses involved, but has improved their value and chance of preservation.

Another contribution was the commissioning of a bust of Charles A. Lindbergh in honor of the Fiftieth Anniversary of his transatlantic flight to Paris. Granville W. Carter, now president of the National Sculpture Society, was chosen once more as sculptor, and the portrait

*An "Apostle" house of 1874, rescued by the Garden City
Historical Society. (Drennan)*

*View of Garden City in 1878 showing "A. T. Stewart Era
Buildings."*

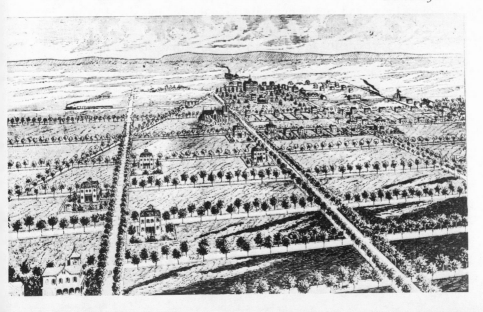

in bronze, unveiled at the Nassau County's Lindbergh Celebration in 1977, has already won several medals and awards. It is now on loan in the Garden City Public Library.

A welcome addition to the Village was the Senior Citizen Recreation Center on Golf Club Lane — a small, intimate building made possible by the allocation of Federal Revenue Sharing Funds. A haven for the Retired Men's Club, it also became popular with women's groups, duplicate bridge addicts, and shuffleboard enthusiasts. The golf clubs, Casino, playgrounds, and swimming pool have also continued to provide assorted recreation in the Village, but a proposed indoor Ice-Skating Rink was turned down by referendum vote.

Recreation and retirement for George Loring Hubbell, Jr., had a special meaning to Garden City in 1975. Although he would continue to play golf and bridge, he had decided to retire from the position of Village Counsel, which he had held for fifty-five years. Starting in 1920 as a young lawyer and one of the 2,140 residents of the newly-incorporated Village, he had helped to guide it through its growing pains, its achievements, its problems and dangers to its maturity as a successful and outstanding community of over 25,000 residents.

The big event of the decade was the Bicentennial Celebration of 1976, which lasted from September to July with seemingly unabated enthusiasm. This was partly due to the Gala Ball and Buffet Dinner, which launched the festivities in the unique setting of a huge red-and-white candy-striped tent on top of Bloomingdale's three-story parking facility. The organizers, fearful of a possible September hurricane, had small holes bored through the flat roof and guy wires placed to keep the spectacular monster from flying off into space. Chairs, tables, bars, and platforms were brought up the spiral ramps by truck, and the huge circus roof was decorated with flags and bunting. The 1,200 residents and guests who came that night will probably never forget the party even though no storm occurred.

The next months of celebration produced a big dinner at the Casino, a craft show, a Pictorial Exhibition of Early Garden City at the Library, and, as spring arrived, another unusual event — Colonial Day. For once Seventh Street became a pedestrian mall for a giant block party which attracted thousands of residents and visitors. Early summer heralded picnics and parades, capped on July 4 by the final event of the year-long celebration — an Ecumenical Service with Archbishop Fulton J. Sheen as speaker.

Another gratifying feature of the year had been the visit of a group from Coburg, Germany, resulting, three years later, in a return visit by one from Garden City which further cemented the friendship between the two sister cities. International relations through the Student Exchange continued, greatly enhanced by the invitation to the High School Band to take part in the Queen's Silver Jubilee Parade in London, and by the visit of the Cathedral Choir to join in services at three of England's great cathedrals. To encourage cultural exchange between its American and foreign students, Adelphi University established "International House" in 1979 as part of the Fiftieth Anniversary Celebration of its move to Garden City. Other events followed, highlighted by a ground-breaking ceremony for a large addition to its Library.

In spite of inflation and general austerity, another building project started that year on a seven-acre site on Franklin Avenue and Kellum Place. Called the "Franklin Avenue Office Center" by its developer, Thomas Pepitone of Pepitone Industries, it already promises to be one of Long Island's largest and most striking office complexes — with its four unusual contemporary buildings, multilevel parking facilities, and its resourceful site plan.

This new "Center" and earlier Franklin Avenue projects in the area zoned for business development, combined with the various public buildings of the County Seat, have made Garden City a center of commercial, office, and civic construction on Long Island and have helped it to maintain a high credit rating. This fiscal stability, along with a reasonable level of taxation, high quality services, an orderly government, a new Library and good schools, a University, and a beautiful Cathedral, all bear out a recent poll's designation of Garden City as one of America's most distinguished communities.

ACKNOWLEDGMENTS

A local history is never the product of one person's efforts. It repre-
sents the help, generosity and co-operation of many, and this story of
Garden City is no exception. The author wishes to thank everyone
who has made the book possible—from librarians, businessmen,
artists, photographers, and historians in other fields, to local schools,
churches, organizations, Village officials, and long-time residents.
More specific acknowledgments for the illustrations follow.

The Locomotive "Post Boy," Irwin Smith; Alexander Turney
Stewart, from the original painting in the Garden City Public Library;
Railroad Station and Train, 1873, from the Long Island Railroad
collection; Early Garden City and Garden City Estates, courtesy of
Mrs. Anne Townsend McKellar and the late George L. Hubbell; Mrs.
Alexander Turney Stewart, from the original painting in the Cathedral School of St. Mary; The Cathedral under Construction, courtesy of Rev. Harold F. Lemoine; Panorama of Garden City, 1884,
courtesy of Robert D. Harrower; Cornerstone Laying of St. Paul's,
from *Leslie's Illustrated Weekly*; St. Paul's as a Military School, from
the collection of the Cathedral School of St. Paul; Map of Old Garden City, from Wolverton's *Atlas of Queen's County*, 1891; Queen's
County Agricultural Society, from W. W. Munsell's *History of*

Queen's County; Hunt Club Meet at Garden City Hotel, from *The Daily Graphic*; Vanderbilt Cup Race, courtesy of Henry Austin Clark, Jr.; Parkway Toll House, photograph by Wendell Kilmer; Gold Bug Hotel and Curtiss Engineering Plant, courtesy of Nassau County Museum; Early Aviation in Garden City, photographs by Joseph Burt; Theodore Roosevelt Laying Cornerstone, from Doubleday & Co., Inc.; Camp Mills, 1917, from U. S. War Department, National Archives; Later Camp Mills, courtesy of Mrs. Charles E. Clark; Lindbergh and Chamberlin at Garden City Hotel, from collection of Garden City Public Library; Endpaper maps, Stewart Purchase of the Plains, from *Harper's Weekly*, 1869, and Garden City, reproduced from the official map of Garden City.

BIBLIOGRAPHY

Bassett, Preston R., *Long Island, Cradle of Aviation*, Long Island Forum, Amityville, N. Y., 1950.

Curtiss, Glenn H. and Augustus Post, *The Curtiss Aviation Book*, Frederick A. Stokes Co., New York, 1912.

Denton, Daniel, *Brief Description of New York, Formerly Called New Netherlands, with the Places Thereunto Adjoining*, London, 1670; reprint, with notes by Gabriel Furman, published by William Gowans, New York, 1845.

Dwight, Timothy, *Travels in New England and New York*, Vol. III; New Haven, 1822.

Floyd-Jones, Thomas, *Backward Glances*; published by the author, New York, 1914.

Gabriel, Ralph Henry, *The Evolution of Long Island*, Yale University Press, 1921.

Garden City News, The (a newspaper), 1923-1963.

Garden City, Village of, *Annual Reports*, 1931-1962.

—————— Zoning Ordinance No. 29, adopted March 7, 1924. Garden City Public Library.

Hubbell, George L., personal scrapbook, 1893-1900; unpublished. Garden City Public Library.

Lessner, Erwin Christian, *Famous Auto Races and Rallies*, Hanover House, 1956.

Moore, Rev. William H., *History of St. George's Church, Hempstead,* E. P. Dutton, New York, 1881.

Newspapers, 1869-1963, including *The Brooklyn Daily Eagle, Harper's Weekly, The Hempstead Sentinel, Leslie's Illustrated Weekly, The Nassau Daily Review-Star, The New York Sun,* and *The New York Times.*

Peters, Ralph, "The Long Island Railroad in the War, 1917-1919." In typescript; unpublished. Garden City Public Library.

Posthumous Relatives of the Late Alexander T. Stewart: Proceedings before the Surrogate and excerpts from newspapers, 1876. New York Public Library.

Randall, C. Walter, "Garden City: Its Incorporation as a Village and Its Community Agreement"; pamphlet, 1954.

Reifschneider, Felix E., "History of the Long Island Railroad," in Hazelton's *The Boroughs of Brooklyn and Queens, the Counties of Nassau and Suffolk,* Vol. I, pp. 384-420; New York, 1925.

Resseguie, Harry E., Biography of A. T. Stewart, as yet unpublished. "The Decline and Fall of the Commercial Empire of A. T. Stewart," *Harvard Business History Review,* Fall 1962.

Ross, Peter, *A History of Long Island,* Lewis Publishing Company, New York, 1903.

Schultz, Bernice, *Colonial Hempstead,* Review-Star Press, Lynbrook, N. Y., 1937.

Seyfried, Vincent F., *New York and Long Island Traction Company;* published by the author, 1952.

Shanks, Major General David C., *As They Passed Through the Port,* Chapter XXII; Cary Publishing Company, Washington, D. C., 1927.

Smith, Louise Carter, "Long Island Motor Parkway," *Nassau County Historical Journal,* Vol. XXII (Spring 1961).

Smits, Edward J., *The Creation of Nassau County,* Mineola, 1960.

Thompson, Benjamin F., *History of Long Island,* Third Edition; Robert H. Dodd, New York, 1918.

Tredwell, Daniel N., *Personal Reminiscences of Men and Things on Long Island,* G. P. Putnam's Sons, New York, 1924.

Walling, George W., *Recollections of a New York Chief of Police,* Caxton Book Concern, New York, 1887.

Werner, Charles J., *Historical Miscellanies Relating to Long Island,* Huntington, N. Y., 1927.

Youngs, Mary Fanny, "History of the Cathedral of the Incarnation," unpublished. Garden City Public Library.

INDEX

On August 7, 1869, Harper's Weekly printed this map showing location of the 7,000 acres (shaded) of the Hempstead Plains purchased by Mr. A. T. Stewart. The white area indicates the general outline of Garden City.

The official map of present-day Garden City.

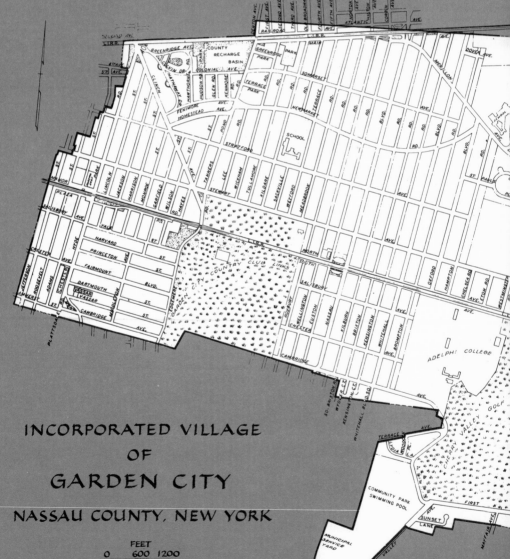

INCORPORATED VILLAGE
OF
GARDEN CITY
NASSAU COUNTY, NEW YORK

FEET
0   600   1200
GRAPHIC SCALE